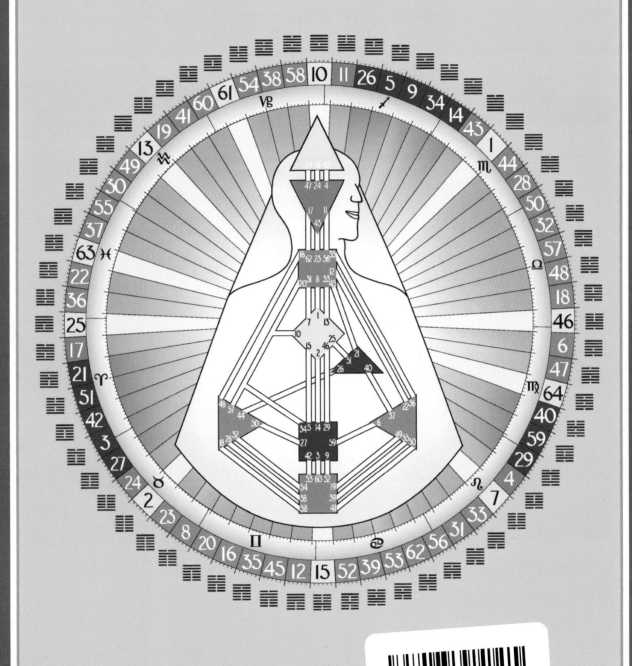

Get your Free, or Full Personal Report, including your
Human Design Life Chart from :

www.HumanDesignForUsAll.com

or from :

www.TheSuccessTransformation.com/human-design-reports/

Download Your Free Software now to draw up charts from:
www.HumanDesignForUsAll.com/free-software
This software is for Windows-based computers and can be run on Apple/Mac computers with crossover software. (Like Parallels or Fusion).

Or through the Mac Bootcamp with any Windows OS.

Get your Free, or Full Personal Report including your Human Design Life Chart from:
www.HumanDesignForUsAll.com

THE BOOK OF LINES

A 21st Century View of the
IChing,
the Chinese Book of Changes

CHETAN PARKYN

ISBN–978-1-5076-8718-5

Also available in Bulgarian through Millenium Publishers (ISBN 978-954-515-211-5)

Cover design by Sally Taylor – Represented by Artist Partners www.artistpartners.com
Interior design by The Set Up Graphics, www.thesetugraphics.com

Also by this author :

Human Design, Discover the Person You Were Born To Be

Harper Collins, UK. www.HarperCollins.co.uk (ISBN 978-0-00-728124-4)
New World Library, USA. www.NewWorldLibrary.com (ISBN 978-1-57731-941-2)

World language editions :
Butik Yayincilik, Turkey. www.butikyayincilik.com (978-605-552-423-4
Natural Spirit, Japan. www.naturalspirit.co.jp (ISBN 978-4-86451-003-5
Millenium Bblishers , Bulgaria. (ISBN 978-954-515-188-0)
Acorn Publishing, Taiwan. (ISBN 978-986-6362-74-3)
Her One Media, South Korea. (ISBN 978-89-92162-62-3)
Acorn International Publishing Ltd., Taiwan. (ISBN 978-986-6362-74-3)
Kamphausen Mediengruppe, Germany. (ISBN 978-3-89901-849-3)

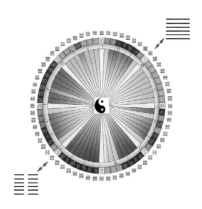

This book is dedicated to Carola Eastwood (Deva Nishtha), whose Divine Trust has extended most generously to loving, supporting and traveling with me in this wonder-filled life journey.

There is a music which has no sound;
The soul is restless for such music.

There is love in which the body is not;
The soul longs for such unembodied love.

There is a truth which has no form;
The soul longs for this formless truth.

Therefore melodies do not satisfy;
Bodies do not satisfy
And forms cannot fulfill the soul

But this lack of fulfillment,
This dissatisfaction,
Has to be understood properly,
For such understanding ultimately brings about transcendence.

Then sound becomes the door to the soundless,
The body becomes the path to the unembodied,
And form becomes the formless.

Osho,
from the book, *A Cup of Tea.*

CONTENTS

FOREWORD

Having enjoyed the privilege of traveling through life with Chetan Parkyn as his business partner and wife, but most importantly, as his friend, my soul has been deeply touched by the huge heart, wit, and wisdom, of this beautiful and talented man. Over the years, I discovered more and more the authentic love he has for everyone, and the depth of spiritual insight and wisdom he is capable of conveying to us all. The huge gift that Chetan has is his ability to speak through the symbols reflected in one's life, to address your heart and soul in a way that leaves one forever, "touched" by his clear reflection and startling insights.

For more than a decade, Chetan daily spent hours and hours and hours, pouring over all the elements he knew of Human Design. It was through this process of testing, discovering, and refining the work, that he identified the specific key elements of Human Design that emerged as the central most important factors to share with others; those elements that would assist in awakening one's authentic self. My enthusiasm for his work with Human Design grew as I watched him gain greater and greater mastery over the art of delivering a highly impactful personal reading, and as I watched him for years, developing and refining his teaching materials for those seeking to learn about Human Design.

More and more people's lives began changing significantly as we refined our understanding of Human Design and he refined his methods of conveying the multi-layered nuances of meaning in a Human Design Life Chart. Having had a long career giving astrology readings, I was amazed at the depth, accuracy, and reach of Human Design, with its profound ability to awaken people to their authentic self and help us move through life with clarity and effectiveness in all that we do. I was fascinated to find that not only the conscious self, but the unconscious, inherited patterns from generations past, were also contained within ones' Human Design, and could be read and understood! But my greatest learning, and highest benefit came as I began incorporating Human Design into my way of daily living and relating.

A central part of Chetan's research was into one of the elements contained within Human Design, the *I Ching*, from which is drawn a symbolic understanding of the message contained within each of the 64 Hexagrams, which relate to the 64 genetic codons in our human make-up. As you may imagine, the nuances of meaning derived from the encoded information passed down from previous generations is complex. Chetan was inspired to interpret these symbols for us in ways that would shed the greatest light on our journey. I've lost count of how many revisions he has written, but over the course of twelve years, I watched him evolve the language, bringing deeper insight and refining it with each re-write. His dedication to getting his Book of Lines to the point where it would most fully reflect the authentic meaning of each of the Hexagrams, and indeed, each of the 384 lines within the hexagrams seemed inexhaustible; so much so that I was truly surprised one day when he announced it completed.

In his first book, Human Design, Discover the Person You Were Born to Be, Chetan introduced us to the art and science of self-discovery that is revealed by knowing your Human Design. The Book of Lines is written both as a companion to his Human Design book, but also, as a stand-alone modern-day interpretation of the ancient Chinese text, the *I Ching*. Levels and levels of personal insight are contained within the symbolic language of *The Book of Lines*. Use it to read through all of the 26 activations in your Human Design Life Chart to get a profound and coherent symbolic picture of the person you were born to be and life you were born to live. Use it also, to consult about any area of your life that you wish to shed more light upon, and you will be given answers that uncannily speak to the heart of your question, giving you broader insight into your life journey. Let *The Book of Lines* become one of those treasures on your bookshelf that you refer to frequently over the years.

Carola Eastwood,
Professional Astrologer and Success Coach

ACKNOWLEDGEMENTS

I wish to acknowledge all those who have trusted me to read for them, and who have provided insights that have been woven into this book.

Without the presence of Osho in my life, it is hard for me to imagine what an alternative would be.

My great thanks and acknowledgement go to Ra Uru Hu as the one who had the tenacity to withstand downloading Human Design, and who opened the doorway to introduce Human Design as the first International Language to the world.

Sincere thanks go to Alexander Roberts (www.thesetupgraphics.com) who has helped me to maintain the vision for this book, and also patiently, and again more patiently produced the extraordinary graphics and layout.

In the many years of playing with the *IChing*, I have read and reread many different interpretations of this remarkable Book of Changes in an attempt to distill the inner meanings hidden within the codes and images of our lives. I do not consider myself a scholar of the *IChing*, but someone who has received great support, encouragement and guidance from the wisdom contained within it, and I am grateful for everyone who has gone before me in exploring and giving color and interpretation to this amazing body of knowledge.

For those who have an expansive appetite to explore more deeply into this knowledge and the realms of the *IChing*, I direct your attention to my great friend, Richard Rudd's book: *Gene Keys* (ISBN : 978-0578038551)

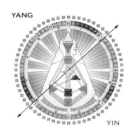

OUTLINE

The Book of Lines gives access to the *IChing, the Chinese Book of Changes*, in Twenty-first Century language that is specifically tailored towards Human Design. This book is written as a companion to my first book: *Human Design, Discover the Person You Were Born To Be.*

The Book of Lines can also be employed by those seeking to use it as a divination device, to foresee or get greater appreciation in their life journey at any particular moment in time.

Additionally, it also can be used by Astrologers seeking to find more specific meaning to particular parts of the Heavens around us and how the planets of our Solar system behave there.

Truth cannot be expressed in words, but words can lead you towards the truth....if you let them ...... and then leave them ......

INTRODUCTION

In 1979, in India, in my early days with the Enlightened Spiritual Master Osho in Poona, I was given an English language version of Richard Wilhelm's German translation of the Chinese *IChing*. I found myself watching my "unconscious" become apparent as it was described in abstract language from an ancient culture that saw life in a very different way than what I was accustomed to experiencing. I was riveted, and started an erratic study of the implications of "throwing" the *IChing* and watching its predictions "unfold" in my life. It was an extraordinary experience as anyone who has studied or "played with" the *IChing* will have found.

Inspired to know more about myself, and the world I found myself in, I visited a celebrated Chhayashastri (Shadow Reader) in Mumbai, who among many things, predicted that I would spend my life reading for people. After he had invited me to come study with him, and I had innocently declined having no idea that I was being given an extraordinary invitation by a world authority, he told me that a system was going to come into my life, that I would introduce to people all over the world, and affect their lives in a profound way. He advised me to start practicing reading for people, to choose any means to find out how to introduce people to themselves through what I saw. He suggested I look into any and all esoteric and other ways of reading people so I would be ready for when the "new system" would appear in my life.

Life with the Enlightened Master Osho always brings transformation in full measure, and within a week, I was approached by a celebrated Indian Psychic Palmist who showed me how to start reading hands… and so the doors opened into many years of reading hands, faces, tarot, astrology, runes, tealeaves and many other means of looking into everyone's lives. Through the ensuing years, the *IChing* was always very close to my heart because it provided a means to put an array of sensations and experiences into words.

In 1993, I was sent my Human Design chart by an old friend… and I had the immediate recognition that this was the system the Master Chhayashastri had foretold. All the pieces of my study and practice with esoteric systems fell into place, and I started practicing earnestly getting to grips with Human Design.

Human Design

Human Design had been "downloaded" by a Canadian man called Ra Uru Hu (now deceased) in January 1987, in very arduous circumstances. I use the word "downloaded" rather than "channeled" because Ra was forced to absorb the system by what he described as the "Voice." Ra's "download" experience continued for 8 days and nights, and did not sound like fun. He described the intelligence that gave him the information of the Human Design as being far beyond anything he had imagined to be possible. At the end of the "download" he found himself with an amazing system but without any instructions of what to do with it!

Human Design is composed, or synthesized from four ancient wisdom traditions as well as two modern-day sciences. The ancient wisdoms are (Western) Astrology as the means to find the placements and meaning of heavenly bodies around us; the Kaballah and particular an understanding of the branches of Tree of Life; the Chakras or energy centers in the body; and the *IChing, The Chinese Book of Changes*. The modern-day sciences are an understanding of neutrinos as the tiny "messengers" of the Universe, and the Human Genetic coding and how we describe our experience of life in human form.

A direct link between the 64 Hexagrams of the *IChing* and the 64 Human Genetic codons was established by the German physician, Dr Martin Schonberger in 1973 (*IChing and the Genetic Code: The Hidden Key to Life*). So, if you are able to comprehend what the Hexagrams of the *IChing* represent and how to describe them, you can also comprehend and actually "read" what the psychological genetic makeup is in any individual. Contained within the codes of your Human Design are ancestral streams of experiences and distilled wisdom which are embedded in your "psycho-spiritual DNA." By understanding your unique genetic makeup expressed in clear language, you have access to the keys to your life.

This book is the result of many years practice with the *IChing*, many re-writes and fine-tunings to find clear language that expresses many of the nuances of the *IChing* and hence our inherent genetic tendencies!

HOW TO USE THIS BOOK

The Book of Lines has been deliberately written as a sequence of "sutras," or "koans," or "threads of concepts" becoming sequences of words that are tied to particular parts of our human makeup. If you can be receptive and allow the knowledge to "land" in your awareness, these "threads of concepts" are sequences of words that lead you into profound understanding of yourself and those around you.

The 64 hexagrams are found to align exactly with the 64 "codons" of Human Genetics. The Book of Lines offers the possibility to have an experience of each particular aspect of our personal genetics through finding a personal resonance with the language used to describe them.

Please consider these written lines to be "triggers" or "keys" as guidance for introspection, contemplation or meditation, rather than, or at least as a combination with, just pieces of information.

We are here to live life in all its shapes and forms, and the Book of Lines can give you access to intrinsic parts of your nature as a personal experiencing of who you are, and what you are here living out, and how you are evolving. You will notice that the Lines, for the most part, have been deliberately written in present tense, and directly to you.

If you do not have your Human Design Life Chart, you may access yours, free of charge, by going to **www.HDFUA.com** *or* **www.HumanDesignForUsAll.com** *and either download the free software, or put in your Birth information (Date, Place and Time of Birth) and have your Personal Report containing your Life Chart, delivered to you by email.*

How to read the Lines in a Life Chart

If the details below appear at first glance too complex, please rest assured that you can derive meaning about the process of your life without understanding each of the nuances described here. As you read further, you will find a simple explanation about how to use this book as a guide to understanding the broader scope of your life experience.

Here is an example of two facing pages and the items on them:

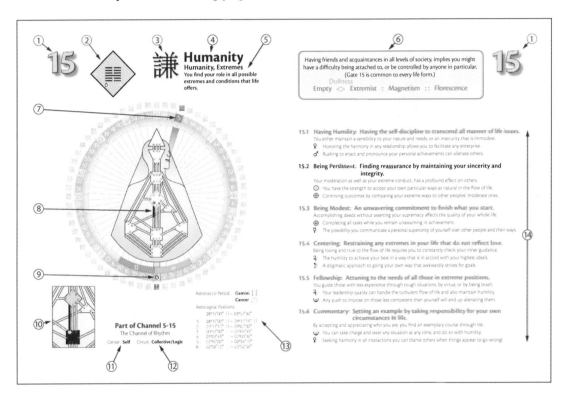

1. Gate Number
2. Hexagram
3. Chinese Character
4. Gate Name
5. Gate Meaning
6. Commentary
7. Other Hexagram defining Channel 5 -15

8. Gate in the Life Chart
9. Hexagram in the Wheel
10. Gate as part of Channel 5-15
11. Gate in Center
12. Gate in Circuit
13. Astrological Degrees of Lines
14. The Lines from 1 through 6.

Each Gate has a Number, ①, and a Hexagram, ②, that is made up of "Chop marks." The

Chop Marks are either "solid" marks, ——————— , that are described as "Yang," Male, Outgoing, Creative energy, or "broken" marks, ——— ——— , that are described as "Yin," Female, Ingoing, or Receptive.

Each Hexagram has a Chinese Character, or Pictogram that relates to it, ③.

Each Gate has a Name,④, a Meaning,⑤, that gives a brief description of how it operates, and a Commentary, ⑥, that describes its broader effect in the world.

Each Gate has a specific place in the Life Chart, ⑧.

Each Hexagram has a specific place in the Wheel, ⑨, and has the potential correspondence with another Hexagram, ⑦. When these two Hexagrams are activated, they make up a "defined" Channel in the Life Chart, ⑩.

Each Gate is in one of the 9 Centers, ⑪, and is placed in one of the major Circuits that run through the Life Chart, ⑫.

Each Gate corresponds to a Hexagram that has a specific placement in the sky, or the starfields around us that can be shown by exact degrees, minutes and seconds of arc in Astrological terms, ⑬.

There are 6 Lines in each Gate, and each has a specific description and role to play in life, ⑭. Ultimately, each Line in a Gate relates to the Hexagram, portion of Starfield and Genetic Codon within our makeup of consciousness in form.

How to apply the descriptions of Gates and Lines to a Life Chart

Each Life Chart has two calculations for placements in the sky around us of the Sun, the Moon, the Nodes and each of the Planets in our Solar System. The calculations are recorded in Hexagram and Line Number. Here is an example for the "conscious" and "unconscious" Sun, ☉, and Earth, ⊕ :

$$\text{Unconscious} \quad \text{Conscious}$$
$$41^1 \ ☉ \ 3^5$$
$$31^1 \ ⊕ \ 50^5$$

One calculation is made for the moment of birth, and the Hexagram and Line Numbers are recorded in **black**, indicating that these are "conscious" aspects of our nature that we will recognize in ourselves.

The second calculation is made for a moment 88 degrees of Solar Arc, or approximately 3 months before birth while we are still in the womb. These Hexagram and Line Numbers are recorded in pink, indicating that they are an "unconscious" part of our makeup. Premature or late births use this same calculation.

"Traditionally" this "unconscious" aspect has been explored through psycho-analysis, hypnotism and other forms of therapy. The significance of the "unconscious" pink information is that it relates to our genetic inheritance that comes from parents, their parents and at least 4 generations of input, and through Human Design becomes immediately apparent. What can be deduced from examining Human Design is that we are given direct access to our "genetic inheritance." This is not to say that any gifts or poor personal attitudes are "due to my ancestors," but it does give us a new level of understanding of our journey to be more conscious about how we are in our life.

Reading the Gates and Lines

In the example above for the Conscious Sun, $\odot\,3^5$ we would read **Gate 3, and then Line 5.**

This following passages are from *The Book of Lines*, first the gate meaning and commentary, and then Line 5 :

Gate 3. Beginnings: Implementing the New: In breaking with old ways, clear perspective, perseverance and some principles of organizing are needed. Tradition does not easily give way to the new, the unknown and untried.

The **Gate 3** meaning informs you that you are living a life in which you are breaking with traditions and establishing new and previously untried ways. Below is the entire text for Gate 3, Line 5, not all of which may erlate to your life.

3.5 **Interpreting: Detaching from anticipated results when implementing a new order.**
In organizing anything new, there is the possibility of your intentions being misinterpreted.
♂: Your assured individual stance withstands any disagreements and establishes order.
⊕: You can easily become confused in your attempts to reconcile others' problems.

Since the Line is activated by the Sun, $\odot$, we read the first two lines and not those that are particular to Mars, ♂, or the Earth, ⊕.

3.5 **Interpreting: Detaching from anticipated results when implementing a new order.**
In organizing anything new, there is the possibility of your intentions being misinterpreted.

The Gate 3, Line 5 meaning indicates that you cannot expect to know exactly how things are going to turn out when implementing your new approaches to life, nor can you expect everyone to appreciate exactly what you are doing. You might find yourself "making things up as you go along," and hoping you "get away with it."

In this same example, for the Conscious Earth, ⊕, we read from *The Book of Lines* **Gate 50, Line 5.**

First : **Gate 50 : Values: Stability:** Honoring the wisdom and being responsible for values that enrich both local community and society at large. Spiritual and earthly powers are joined by taking responsibility to hold and promote values of merit that are traditional or novel, but which are relevant to the essential needs of any moment.

The Gate 50 meaning indicates that you are responsible to uphold values for the people around you according to what is actually needed.

Then :

50.5   **Enhancing: Maintaining alertness to recognize which values serve best.**
You recognize or disregard a correlation between the values and actions that serve everyone.
♄: You grow wise enough to uphold appropriate values when pressured to change them.
♂: In a rush to get on in life, you can disregard the real values that serve yourself and others.

Since the Line is activated by the Earth, ⊕, we read the first two lines and not those that are particular to Saturn, ♄, or Mars, ♂.

The Gate 50, Line 5 meaning indicates that you are alert to changing values, and might have to shift from what you consider are "right" values, to those that are actually serving people in any particular instance.

******

For the Unconscious Sun, ☉, we read **Gate 41, Line 1,**

First, **Gate 41, Imagination: Evaluating Potentials:** Living within limiting resources gives occasion for dreams and fantasies to arise. In the search to be fulfilled you look into any potential experiences that might move your through a cycle from emptiness to accomplishment. Dreaming opens doorways to experiences that bring satisfaction and completion, or endless fantasies that are self-sustaining. Existence was created when we fell in love with emptiness.

Then :

41.1   **Moderating: Finding the balance between giving and receiving.**
Being either centered and clear, or headstrong in your handling of how you use your energies.
♆: Your creative imagination streams resources in ways that benefit yourself and others.
☿: Confusion with your role and resources leads you into difficulties at the outset of endeavors.

The unconscious Gate 41 meaning indicates that as an unconscious undercurrent, you have a vivid imagination that explores many possibilities in life…some of which might become a reality, and some just a fantasy.

The unconscious Gate 41, Line 1 indicates that as an unconscious undercurrent, you need to find the happy medium between what you can realistically expect to offer to, and receive from life.

******

And for the Unconscious Earth, ⊕, we read **Gate 31, Line 1**

First, **Gate 31, Influence: "I lead….because…."** : Mutual attractions and your readiness to interrelate allow you to express your natural influence. The potential to provide guidance and instruction align you and others with future prospects. It is important to relate from your own independent vision of reality.

Then :

31.1 Opening: Finding the sincerity to allow yourself to be influential.
You either offer your ideals in simple ways or through contrived means.
⊙: You express leadership through clear alignment with your inherent aims.
⊕: Attempting to establish influential roles you might align with status rather than ideals.

The unconscious Gate 31 meaning indicates that as an unconscious undercurrent you have an air around you that affects others to want to pay attention to you…..if you will allow for it, and stay true to your own nature.

The unconscious Gate 31, Line 1 has a part that relates particularly to the Earth, ⊕ so we are going to read the top line (in blue) and then the line that is next to the Earth, ⊕ symbol :
The top (blue) line indicates that you have an unconscious undercurrent that grows over time when you recognize more and more that everyone pays attention to you because what you say and do is influencing them.
The Earth, ⊕, activation indicates that as an unconscious undercurrent you tend to be interested in influencing or upholding the apparent ordering of a class structure around you.

…….and you do this for all the Gates and Lines in your Chart, one by one, slowly, and paying attention to the sense each sentence or phrase is relaying to you, in both your conscious and unconscious.

When a Line has blue writing, it is an indication that the potential wisdom inherent in the Line develops and grows during the lifetime.

When a Line has black writing, it indicates that the quality of the meaning is set from birth.

Some lines are ▐highlighted pink▌ with either Pluto (ʬ) or Neptune (Ψ), the two slowest orbiting planets, indicating that no one alive now, in 2012, (in a "normal" lifespan) has that particular activation in their chart......... These activations would apply to past or future generations, and "generational influences" relating to those times.

Some lines are highlighted yellow , indicating that either Neptune or Pluto has recently, or is very close to, activating that line for the first time in an aeon. (248 years for Pluto, 165 years for Neptune)...

Further study

The **words colored in green** in the Gate Commentary are from Richard Rudd's book *GeneKeys, Unlocking the Higher Purpose Hidden in Your DNA* (www.Genekeys.co.uk).

Richard examines what he calls "The Gifts."... and describes the range of consciousness from a low-level frequency (Introvert < > Extrovert) to a high level frequency (: Gift :: Realization) associated with each Hexagram/Genekey.

The "Gift" or trigger recognition that takes us from low-level frequency to realization is the third word along in each row of words.

Hovering over the "Introvert" ⬦ "Extrovert" low-level range of frequencies of each Key is what Richard calls the "Shadow" element that holds us back in our wish to grow and evolve in consciousness.

For Example :

Gate 2. Receptivity

Dislocation
Lost ⬦ Regimented : Orientation :: Oneness

From low-level frequencies of (introvert) Lost or (extrovert) Regimented, with the sense of Dislocation overshadowing... and by activating the Gift of Orientation you come to the realization of Oneness.

The Planets' glyphs and their energetic influences.

You do not have to know astrology, just be aware of the glyphs for the planets.

☉: **The Sun** (A Star): Dynamic life force, identity, sense of purpose.

⊕: **The Earth:** Grounding, receptivity, the body.

☾: **The Moon** (A Satellite): Reflection, feeling memory, the past.

☊: **North Node:** Your new direction and current life purpose.
(These Nodes are calculated points in Space, and not planets)

☋: **South Node:** Your past-life direction and lessons to assimilate

☿: **Mercury:** Connection to the environment, communication.

♀: **Venus:** Love, beauty, comfort, relationship, yin nature, morals.

♂: **Mars:** Activity, war, aggression, progress, the urge to survive, sex.

♃: **Jupiter:** Expansion, higher learning, philosophic nature.

♄: **Saturn:** Life's lessons, structure, cause/effect, Shadow side.

♅: **Uranus:** Awakening, dramatic change, higher consciousness.

♆: **Neptune:** Unconditional love/confusion/delusion, mystical planes.

♇: **Pluto:** Transformation, death and rebirth at higher levels.

THE
LINES

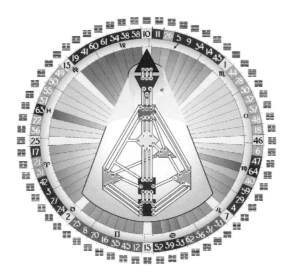

乾 Creativity
Creative Self-expression
Creativity aligns with the natural
expansion of the Universe.

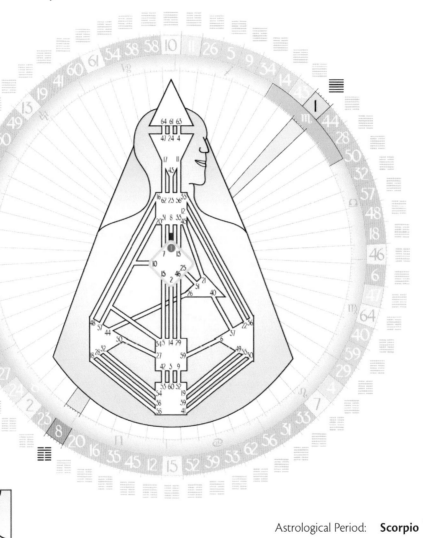

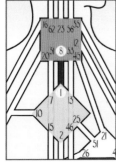

Part of Channel 1-8
Inspiration: The Creative Role Model

Center: **Self** Circuit: **Individual/ Knowing**

Astrological Period: **Scorpio** ♏

Astrological Positions:

13°15'00" ♏ – 18°52'30" ♏

1:	13°15'00" ♏ – 14°11'15" ♏
2:	14°11'15" ♏ – 15°07'30" ♏
3:	15°07'30" ♏ – 16°03'45" ♏
4:	16°03'45" ♏ – 17°00'00" ♏
5:	17°00'00" ♏ – 17°56'15" ♏
6:	17°56'15" ♏ – 18°52'30" ♏

> You open to expand creatively within, through and beyond mundane expressions and into the realms of the extra-ordinary. Aiming innovatively into new forms of co-creation involving anything that life offers.
>
> Entropy
>
> Depressive ◇ Frenetic : Freshness :: Beauty

1.1 Pure Creativity without motive: Gifted with creativity.

Your self-expression is often impulsive and also wholesome when it is effortless.

☾: Reflecting the Moon's phases, your self-expression finds its own natural timing.

⚷: Creative brilliance is hard to restrain. Learning patience is essential for you.

1.2 Being in Accord: Aligning with universal truths.

Creativity is a natural expression always subject to, and altered by your personal agendas.

♀: Creative self-expression intensifies by applying your aspirations and values.

♂: Your full creative potential can be limiting when you express only desires and passions...

1.3 Creative Thrust: Applying yourself to your best ability.

Your creativity is hard to contain and direct, and is affected by any material considerations.

♂: You push for self-expression in all areas of life, regardless of any constraints.

⊕: Materialism invariably affects the quality of your creativity. Being diligent is important.

1.4 The Artist Alone: Finding yourself in the middle of the Creative process.

A flow of personal creativity brings you into intimate contact with Existence.

⊕: Your creativity develops and flowers best away from outside influences.

♃: Trying to influence others directly with your creativity will actually limit it's potential.

1.5 Magnetic Creativity: A means to fascinate people with your creative pursuits.

Your creativity is hard for others to ignore, even if no one grasps what is really happening!

♂: Exuding creativity in every aspect of your life, you naturally fascinate other people.

⚷: Eccentricity may attract attention, but it will eventually limit your truly creative potentials.

1.6 "The Hollow Bamboo": The artist as a medium through whom Existence plays Her song.

Whether you can embrace this or not : creativity is its own resource and the artist the medium.

⊕: Through meditation and detachment you give form to the freest expressions of creativity.

☊: Self-consciousness and seriousness may lead you to be frustrated in your creative endeavors.

2

Receptivity
Guidance
A natural connection exists to unseen and sometimes inexplicable inner guidance.

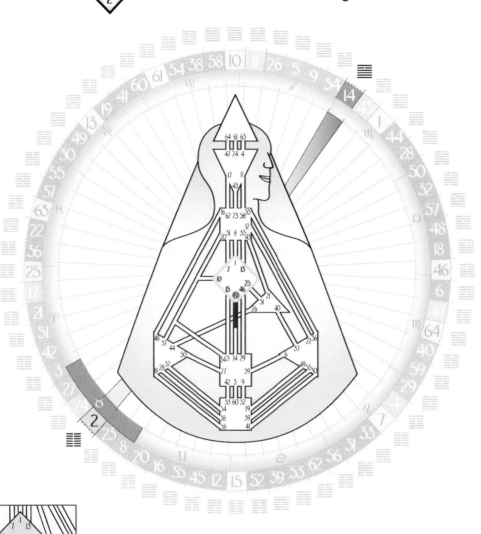

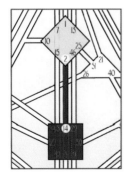

Part of Channel 2-14
Channel of the Alchemist

Center: **Self** Circuit: **Individual/ Knowing**

Astrological Period: **Taurus** ♉

Astrological Positions:

13°15′00″ ♉ – 18°52′30″ ♉

1:	13°15′00″ ♉ – 14°11′15″ ♉
2:	14°11′15″ ♉ – 15°07′30″ ♉
3:	15°07′30″ ♉ – 16°03′45″ ♉
4:	16°03′45″ ♉ – 17°00′00″ ♉
5:	17°00′00″ ♉ – 17°56′15″ ♉
6:	17°56′15″ ♉ – 18°52′30″ ♉

Receptivity provides the means to finding a way through life that is in accord with and guided by the Higher Self. Being Receptive establishes the distinct difference between knowledge and knowing.

Dislocation

Lost ◇ Regimented : Orientation :: Oneness

2.1 Crystal Vision: Receptive to guidance that accords to the beauty of Existence.

Your inner knowing comes through appreciation of the beauty and fragility of life.

♀: You align yourself with high ideals through your sensibility to life.

♂: You try to force predetermined outcomes despite your inborn wisdom.

2.2 Being Gifted: Natural access to an intelligence that often defies logical explanation.

You access an inner sense of knowing beyond the scope of any accumulated knowledge.

♄: Your natural gift for knowing must sooner or later be acknowledged.

♂: With an ability to excel, you tend to seek power through your knowledge.

2.3 Patient knowing: Acknowledging that life never ceases giving lessons.

Aligning within your own particular way brings special rewards, in your own perfect timing.

♃: By being receptive you learn to adapt to every conceivable experience that life offers you.

☋: Your inspiration and powerful sense of knowing is impulsive and often demands expression.

2.4 Concealing: Knowing much but revealing only the essential.

There is universal and learnable knowledge, but some things are impossible to transfer clearly.

♀: Sometimes in the highest interests of harmony your knowledge does not need to be expressed.

♂: A tendency you have to be unable to keep silent brings the likelihood of you causing upset.

2.5 Strategy: Biding your time until action is merited.

You interconnect to every asset life offers, whether others can or need be included or not.

☿: When ready to direct, you communicate clearly and use all available resources wisely.

⊕: A self-centered process leaves you overlooking others and their potential contributions.

2.6 Being Preoccupied: Tunnel Vision limits your capacity to expand fully.

Whether you can embrace this or not : creativity is its own resource and the artist the medium.

☿: Your mind never knows for sure, so it is essential to trust and relax into your own Authority.

♄: 'Security' can become an excuse or 'reason' for everything, even to betray your own ideals.

3

 Beginnings
Implementing the New
In breaking with old ways, clear perspective, perseverance and some principles of organizing are needed.

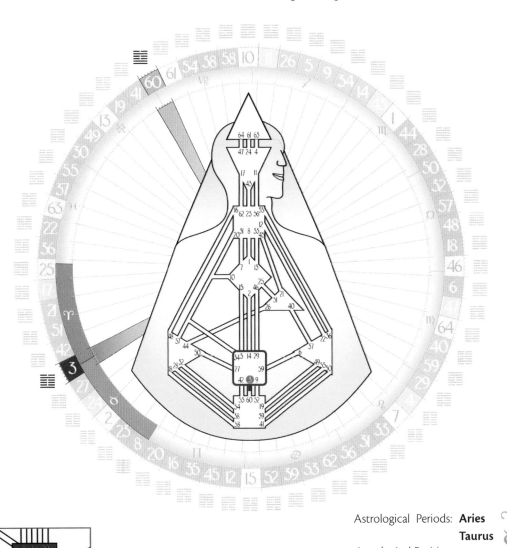

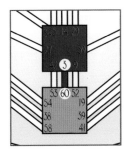

Part of Channel 3-60
The Channel of Mutation

Center: **Sacral**   Circuit: **Individual/ Knowing**

Astrological Periods: **Aries** ♈
                      Taurus ♉

Astrological Positions:
         26°22'30" ♈ – 02°00'00" ♉
1:    26°22'30" ♈ – 27°18'45" ♈
2:    27°18'45" ♈ – 28°15'00" ♈
3:    28°15'00" ♈ – 29°11'15" ♈
4:    29°11'15" ♈ – 00°07'30" ♉
5:    00°07'30" ♉ – 01°03'45" ♉
6:    01°03'45" ♉ – 02°00'00" ♉

Tradition does not easily give way to the new, the unknown and untried.

Chaos

Anal ⬦ Disordered : Innovation :: Innocence

3.1 Being Organized: Embracing the whole picture in front of you.
Confusion is cleared up through your dispassionate review, not through worry and anxiety.
⊕: Trusting that confusion becomes clarity, you keep in sight of all potential outcomes.
☿: Mental muddles will compel you to try many disorganized and scattered endeavors.

3.2 Maturing: Diligent application.
Trusting your own personal evolution, or tending to rely on the advice and ways of others.
♂: You have the potential for personal growth and maturation if you trust your own ways.
⚷: Randomly trusting or disregarding others' advice leads you to a personal instability.

3.3 Scrutinizing: Finding out what works and what does not.
Prospering in life comes about through you recognizing evolutionary laws and their timing.
♀: New ways are more easily introduced when you seek the most able and willing assistance.
☋: If you disregard the law of "survival of the fittest," your ideals will eventually suffer.

3.4 Associating: Realigning with your real sense of purpose
Your self-assurance and trust, or their lack, allow or reject valuable guidance and company.
♆: Your heartfelt attunement with others attracts encouragement and ensures a new order.
♂: If you are impatient in seeking nourishment and guidance you will often be rejected.

3.5 Interpreting: Detaching from anticipated results when implementing a new order.
In organizing anything new, there is the possibility of your intentions being misinterpreted.
♂: Your assured individual stance withstands any disagreements and establishes order.
⊕: You can easily become confused in your attempts to reconcile others' problems.

3.6 Renewing: In all new endeavors remember to keep realigning with your vision.
There is always a potential to get caught up in fear and despair, where orderliness is forgotten.
☉: You have an inner appreciation that ordering is a process that unfolds in its own way.
☋: Forgetting your clear intentions can lead you to become confused and even depressed.

蒙 Mental Solutions

The Pursuit of Answers

Admitting inexperience with any problem
leads to the possibility of finding right
solutions for it.

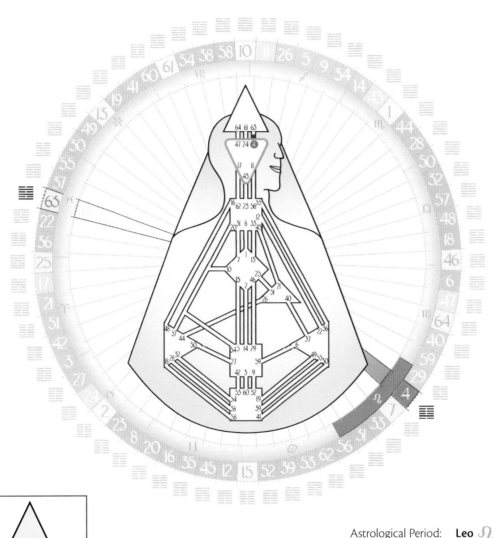

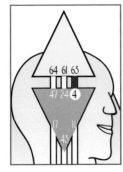

Part of Channel 63-4

Channel of the Logical Mind

Center: **Mind**   Circuit: **Collective/Logic**

Astrological Period: **Leo** ♌

Astrological Positions:

   18°52′30″ ♌ – 24°30′00″ ♌

1:   18°52′30″ ♌ – 19°48′15″ ♌
2:   19°48′45″ ♌ – 20°45′30″ ♌
3:   20°45′00″ ♌ – 21°41′45″ ♌
4:   21°41′15″ ♌ – 22°37′00″ ♌
5:   22°37′30″ ♌ – 23°33′15″ ♌
6:   23°33′45″ ♌ – 24°30′00″ ♌

Being quick with solutions does not necessarily solve problems or lead to lasting satisfaction because most mental solutions are at best partial and temporary.

Intolerance

Apathetic ⬦ Intolerant : Understanding :: Forgiveness

4.1 Learning: Good timing is a gift that enhances solving all problems.
You are always learning the art of recognizing when and where to provide mental solutions.

☾: Acknowledging that profound solutions are available when you really need them.

⊕: You tend to implement resolutions that ignore the natural timing to problem solving.

4.2 Kindness: Recognizing that everyone has their own strengths and weaknesses
Logic can be used in many ways and you may include others in your understandings or not.

☾: You come to appreciate that not everyone is going to understand your viewpoints.

♂: In a hurry, you might sometimes take advantage of other people's slowness and disorder.

4.3 Carelessness: A love of solutions that may not actually solve problems.
If you allow it, a lazy mind will settle for the easiest solution rather than a relevant one.

♀: You have a potential to use solutions for appearances rather than for effectiveness.

☊: Any tendency for diminished responsibility will lead you to meager accomplishments.

4.4 Justifying: A busy mind that somehow is going to find an answer for everything.
You can validate solutions for any scenario, sometimes going beyond any normal level of logic.

☉: You find mental formulas, realistic or not, for every conceivable life situation.

♄: If you try applying mental solutions for everything you'll be frustrated when they don't work!

4.5 Being Broad-minded: Solving difficulties by being open to any and all resources.
With a gift for problem solving you sometimes diminish others' lack of ability to understand.

♃: You have a cleverness for solving problems that is teachable to others.

☊: You are potentially cynical if you have to tailor your solutions to meet others' approval.

4.6 Cleverness: "Too clever for your own good" if you think your mental solutions endure!
Unless disciplined, your mind always tries to dominate life with its solution mechanism.

☿: Mental discipline comes through your patience, awareness and applied experimentation.

♂: You can be arrogant even though you realize the shortcomings of your mental solutions.

5

需 Waiting
Universal timing
All aspects of life have rituals, sequences and timing, both natural and imposed.

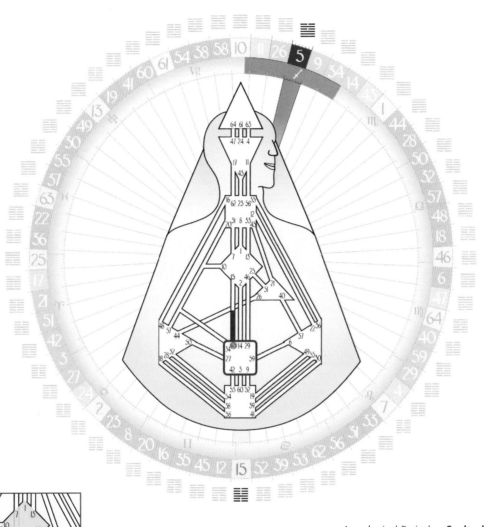

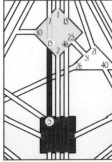

Part of Channel 5-15
The Channel of Rhythm

Center: **Sacral**　　Circuit: **Collective/Logic**

Astrological Period:　**Sagitarius** ♐
Astrological Positions:

	11°22'30" ♐ – 17°00'00" ♐	
1:	11°22'30" ♐	– 12°18'45" ♐
2:	12°18'45" ♐	– 13°15'00" ♐
3:	13°15'00" ♐	– 14°01'15" ♐
4:	14°01'15" ♐	– 15°07'30" ♐
5:	15°07'30" ♐	– 16°03'45" ♐
6:	16°03'45" ♐	– 17°00'00" ♐

> The gardener finds ease in any circumstance by attuning to the natural seasons of change. A potential difficulty working within others' time frames.
>
> Impatience
> Pessimistic ◇ Pushy : Patience :: Timelessness

5.1 Attuning: Persistently paying attention to your own inner timing.

Life is full of distractions that can pull you away from your inherently natural timing.

♂: You have the intent to keep to your own fixed rhythms, regardless of diversions.

⊕: Failing to honor your own timing and giving in to imposed demands brings exhaustion.

5.2 Finding Tranquility: Watchfully waiting for your own right timing.

All actions have an appropriate timing, and you are either comfortable with waiting, or not.

♀: Trusting your own nature to be comfortable with your own pace in all areas of life.

♅: Driving for transformation you suffer anxiety with fixed rhythms and cause disruptions.

5.3 Being Nervous: The potential to become anxious when it seems nothing is happening.

All waiting has an implied helplessness that can prompt you to act without clear motivation.

♆: Your imagination eases the monotony of dull routines and relieves the stress of waiting.

☾: A constantly shifting restlessness upsets your inner timing inclining you to be incautious.

5.4 Biding time: Patience that leaves you open to find worthwhile opportunities.

Watching prevailing conditions and weighing your options until opportunities appear.

⚷: You outlast times of unrest and respond to each situation in life with your innovativeness.

☉: Attempting to force the pace of life, you will lose opportunities in predictable sequences!

5.5   Inner Balancing: Innocent acceptance of life's rhythm is a vital quality of Being.

Seeing what life offers can be a delight, or, if you insist life should bring more, a challenge.

♀: Your inner calm and assurance accepts whatever Existence presents to you.

♅: You may overlook finding joy in simple things and instead adopt demands for change.

5.6 Releasing!: Letting go of any pressures involved in waiting by trusting Universal order.

In all growth, there is pressure. Honoring natural rhythms enables your readiness for response.

♆: By accepting your natural timing, despite pressures, growth will often come through Grace!

♀: You tend to find it hard to release old comforts, lifestyles and relationships.

6

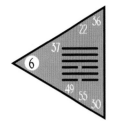

 訟 **Conflict Resolution**

Emotional balance

By dispassionately monitoring changing feelings, the real needs of any moment or situation are recognized. Taking a figurative and literal deep breath.

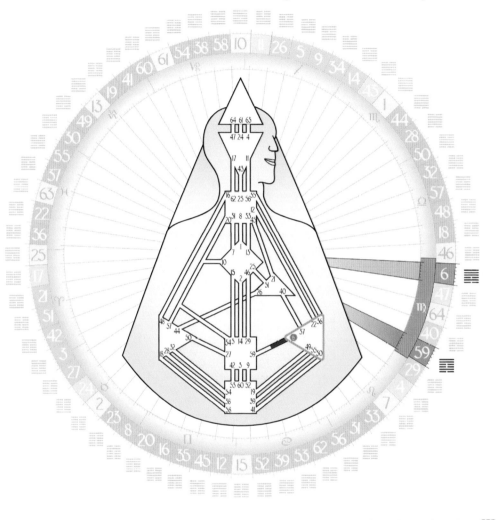

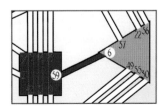

Part of Channel 59-6

The Channel of Connecting

Center: **Emotional**   Circuit: **Tribal/Defense**

Astrological Period: **Virgo** ♍

Astrological Positions:

	22°37'30" ♍ – 28°15'00" ♍
1:	22°37'30" ♍ – 23°33'45" ♍
2:	23°33'45" ♍ – 24°30'00" ♍
3:	24°30'00" ♍ – 25°26'15" ♍
4:	25°26'15" ♍ – 26°22'30" ♍
5:	26°22'30" ♍ – 27°18'45" ♍
6:	27°18'45" ♍ – 28°15'00" ♍

> Emotion is intertwined with and grows in wisdom through intimate
> contact with all aspects of life.
> The body's pH: the internal balance between acidity and alkalinity.
> Conflict
> Overattentive ⬦ Tactless : Diplomacy :: Peace

6.1 Negotiating: The easiest time to resolve a disagreement is before it starts.
With any potential emotional upset, biding your time is often the most intelligent solution.
☋: You have the emotional power and growing maturity to be intimate in all phases of life.
☿: Emotional insecurity in times of intimacy triggers you to attempt to intellectualize feelings.

6.2 Sensibility: Conflicts easily erupt from a personal imbalance.
In all emotionally charged situations, you find resolution with or without confronting others.
♀: Trusting your natural sensitivity you achieve an inner harmony that facilitates resolutions.
♂: Your touchy nature often attempts to resolve conflict through emotional outbursts.

6.3 Having Reservations: Resolutions often happen by playing a passive role.
Achieving emotional clarity comes by making and breaking commitments with alertness.
♆: The depth and quality of your feelings enriches passion, union and intimacy.
☋: Sensitive to all power struggles, you may be tempted to reject intimacy altogether.

6.4 Promoting Peace: A naturally strong emotional presence promotes enduring resolutions.
In all emotional interactions, you can easily promote outcomes on your terms, wisely or not.
☉: You easily dominate relationships and support the advantages of emotional growth.
☋: Personal reform is your only recourse from a tendency to be disruptive in relationships.

6.5 Being Diplomatic: Combining emotional clarity with objectivity.
You promote concord through your neutrality, but find it hard to be really intimate yourself.
♀: Your sensitivity to all facets of emotional upset leads you to promote harmony around you.
☾: Unless you are seen as being 'right,' you can be insensitive to the emotional needs of others.

6.6 Being Contentious: A capacity to win disputes... and attract fresh ones.
You have the knack for resolving emotional upsets whether that directly serves others or not.
☿: You have the emotional agility to resolve conflict by considering everything concerned.
♀: You terminate emotional strife, but often considering only your own needs for harmony.

7

師 **Uniformity**
Finding common intent.
Moving forward in life is made possible through establishing common consent and promoting shared interests among those involved.

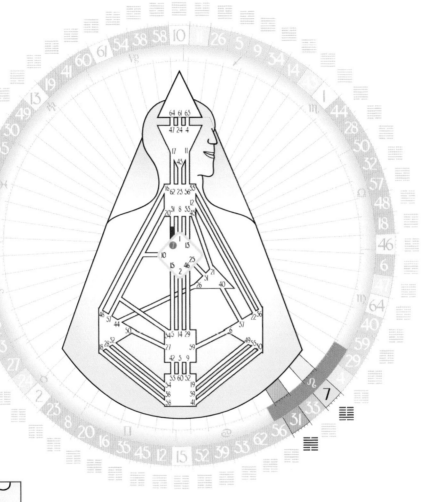

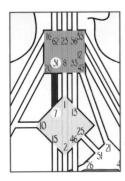

Part of Channel 7-31

The Channel of the Alpha

Center: **Self**   Circuit: **Collective/Logic**

Astrological Period: **Leo** ♌
Astrological Positions:

13°15′00″ ♌ – 18°52′30″ ♌

1:	13°15′00″ ♌ – 14°11′15″ ♌
2:	14°11′15″ ♌ – 15°07′30″ ♌
3:	15°07′30″ ♌ – 16°03′45″ ♌
4:	16°03′45″ ♌ – 17°00′00″ ♌
5:	17°00′00″ ♌ – 17°56′15″ ♌
6:	17°56′15″ ♌ – 18°52′30″ ♌

> In a logical progression, autocracy eventually gives way to democracy,
> and democracy leads ultimately to meritocracy.
>
> Division
> Hidden ◇ Dictatorial : Guidance :: Virtue

7

7.1 Being Discipined: Effective coordination relies on the quality of shared commitments.

Good leadership is achieved through establishing order by making your intentions clear.

♀: You promote coordination and cooperation by launching a friendly yet disciplined course.

☿: Being easily distracted causes you to lose touch with the real needs of any situation.

7.2 Equanimity: Rewards come from implementing any natural advantage.

Your leadership endures through aligning with, or taking advantage of, those you lead.

♆: Being naturally inspirational you give reassurance to those seeking leadership.

☿: You have a potential, once elected, to indulge your self-interest before all other issues.

7.3 Disordering: A reluctance to acknowledge or be drawn in to hierarchies of any sort.

You find order in chaos through playing many, often separating and divergent roles.

☾: You play many varying roles without ever necessarily finding a consistent one.

☿: You can make up reasons to avoid commitment by undermining the purpose in anything.

7.4 Disengaging: Leadership in the highest integrity knows when and how to withdraw.

You are either realistic or not about how your leadership can serve others best.

☉: One of your strengths in leadership is in identifying situations where it is best to withdraw.

☋: Your unwillingness to ever stop advancing will lead eventually to you being abandoned.

7.5 Directing: The confidence and ability to instruct others in the needs of the moment.

As the overall commander, your clear communication in word and deed is essential.

♀: You have the capacity to attract and sustain loyalty by honoring those being led.

♆: You become isolated and ineffective when you fail to focus on real and present needs.

7.6 Meritocracy: Assigning responsibility and guidance to those who merit it.

You remain flexible in using resources well, or become unwilling to lose personal control.

☿: You communicate responsibility in ways that everyone feels included and appreciated.

☋: If you ever communicate responsibility as blame, you will upset the common intent.

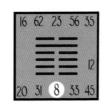

比 **Contribution**
Uniting
Inspiring trust and providing possible
outlets for those who foster and create
novel concepts and ideals.

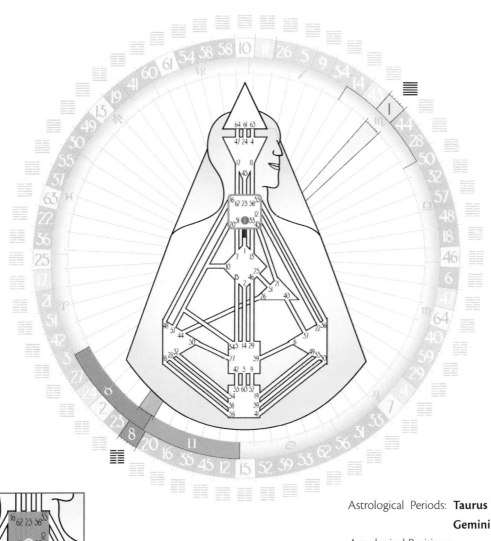

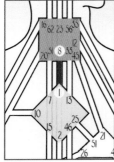

Part of Channel 1-8
Inspiration: The Creative Role Model

Center: **Throat**   Circuit: **Individual/
                                    Knowing**

Astrological Periods: **Taurus** ♉
                                    Gemini ♊

Astrological Positions:
                24°30'00" ♉ – 00°07'30" ♊
1:          24°30'00" ♉ – 25°26'15" ♉
2:          25°26'15" ♉ – 26°22'30" ♉
3:          26°22'30" ♉ – 27°18'45" ♉
4:          27°18'45" ♉ – 28°15'00" ♉
5:          28°15'00" ♉ – 29°11'15" ♉
6:          29°11'15" ♉ – 00°07'30" ♊

Co-creation is realized by the contributions of individuals to promote the personal empowerment of one and all. An agent is the one who often assists others to expand their creativity.

Mediocrity
Mediocre ⬦ Inauthentic : Style :: Exquisiteness

8.1 Being Authentic: Being candid will attract all those who wish to contribute.
Your forthrightness attracts everyone who wishes to engage and co-create with their gifts.

Ψ: You know that your efforts must be offered without concern for obvious rewards.

☿: You compromise your integrity by volunteering randomly and become exploited or spurned.

8.2 Being The Friend: Friendliness is an expression of the highest human ideal.
You naturally empower others through your presence, encouragement and contributions.

☉: Your expression of friendship is intrinsic to your nature.

⊕: Your readiness to contribute has an underlying concern to be recognized and appreciated.

8.3 Indulging: Contributing with a passionate indifference.
You need to constantly check the basis of your commitments and the company you attract.

☾: You express your apparent interest but often without necessarily ever committing yourself.

♄: You rely on techniques to impress others in ways to avoid getting involved with them.

8.4 Being Statesmanlike: Empowering cooperation by welcoming all contributions.
You give heartfelt encouragement to each individual to contribute in their own unique way.

♃: You promote everyone to raise their standards through your contributions and example.

☿: Working "outside the box" your contributions may or may not be appreciated by others.

8.5 Benevolence: Attuning to how, when and what to co-create.
Your timing and attitude assures how well any contribution is received.

♃: Your abundant and kindly manner encourages everyone who is drawn to you.

☉: Your persistent contributing is ultimately appreciated whether you know this or not.

8.6 Reevaluating: Constantly encouraging harmonious environments.
You participate best when you appreciate the vital nature of all empowering contributions.

♀: You comprehend the essence of creative contributions that bring benefits for everyone.

☊: You can become tangled in dramatic personal interactions that result in regrets.

9

小畜 **Applied Details**

Attentiveness

An inherent fascination to examine anything and everything whether it brings ultimate satisfaction or not.

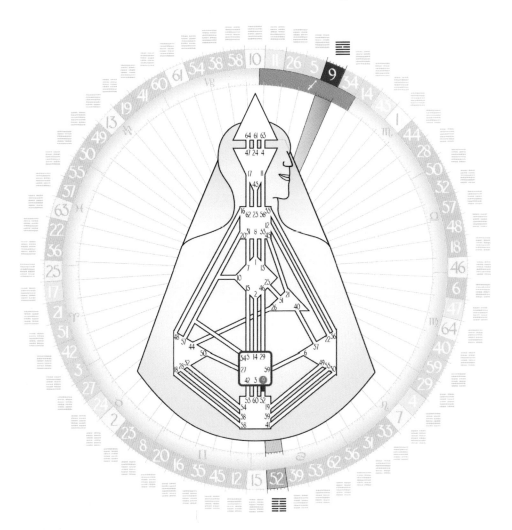

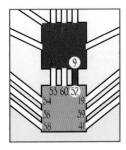

Part of Channel 9-52

The Channel of Concentration

Center: **Sacral**   Circuit: **Collective/Logic**

Astrological Period: **Sagitarius** ♐

Astrological Positions:

05°45′00″ ♐ – 11°22′30″ ♐

1:	05°45′00″ ♐ – 06°41′15″ ♐
2:	06°41′15″ ♐ – 07°37′30″ ♐
3:	07°37′30″ ♐ – 08°33′45″ ♐
4:	08°33′45″ ♐ – 09°30′00″ ♐
5:	09°30′00″ ♐ – 10°26′15″ ♐
6:	10°26′15″ ♐ – 11°22′30″ ♐

Focusing intently so that all the relevant features of our lives
are honored at all times in all our endeavors.

Inertia

Reluctant ⬦ Diverted : Determination :: Invincibility

9.1 Recommencing: Continually reengaging with life from a sense of surety.
You either embrace life's essential details or get frustrated by treating them as problems.

☽: Your intense focus gives you the power to find transformative keys to situations.

♂: You can push past problems, lose your focus and end up being distracted.

9.2 Inclusion: The energy to include and be included.
Your compulsion to collaborate will enhance or distract you from attaining your goals.

☽: You collaborate successfully with others in recognizing fundamental details.

♃: You call on others to play a part in your life and sometimes regret their presence and input.

9.3 Overlooking: Missing the one small but essential detail. Stay focused!
Being distracted you can lose your focus for relevant details, or end up fixating over trivia.

⊕: Doggedly proceeding when you might be better off regrouping and reviewing.

☉: If you constantly obsess over a focus for details you will get poor returns for your efforts.

9.4 Being Dependable: Staying present and focused despite distractions.
Staying true to your intent, or passing over important details, determines your influence in life.

☾: You need determination to act on the relevant details in all phases of a process.

♂: Habitually pushing past essential details, you will eventually succumb to outside pressures.

9.5 Unquestioning: Accomplishment comes through trust and adherence to details.
Accepting life's bounty, or doubting your needs are met, affects your capacity to be fulfilled.

♃: Your contagious power to focus aids in directing attention towards life's essential details.

⊕: A lack of strength to trust yourself aims you towards a growing dissatisfaction with life.

9.6 Being Grateful: The joy and intelligence to celebrate at every opportunity.
By degree, all pressing issues are handled, giving you the space for celebration and relaxation.

☾: Celebrating whenever you get the chance, and especially for any job well done!

☽: You enhance everything by celebrating, especially when you "turn lemons into lemonade."

10

履 **Behavior**

Finding one's place & pace

Empowering behaviors and an attitude of self love triumph amidst all the challenges of life and twists of Fate.

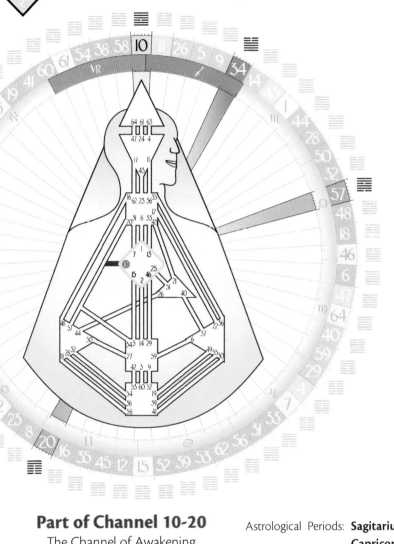

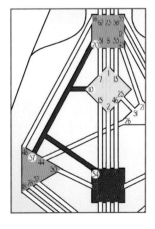

Part of Channel 10-20
The Channel of Awakening

Part of Channel 10-34
The Channel of Exploration

Part of Channel 10-57
The Channel of Survival

Center: **Self**   Circuit: **Individual/ Integration**

Astrological Periods: **Sagitarius** ↗
Capricorn ♑

Astrological Positions:

	28°15'00" ↗ – 03°52'30" ♑
1:	28°15'00" ↗ – 29°11'15" ↗
2:	29°11'15" ↗ – 00°07'30" ♑
3:	00°07'30" ♑ – 01°03'45" ♑
4:	01°03'45" ♑ – 02°00'00" ♑
5:	02°00'00" ♑ – 02°56'15" ♑
6:	02°56'15" ♑ – 03°52'30" ♑

To be fulfilled, your interactions are in accordance with your appreciation and love of life and your singular and precious journey through it.

Self-Obsession

Self-denying ◇ Self-obsessed : Naturalness :: Being

10.1 Investigating: Finding your place in any situation and blending in.
Steady progress in life requires your sensibility to everything you encounter along the way.

⊙: Your honorable behavior in every all situation fosters your growth.

☾: Feeling oversensitive or obligated to others can cause you to avoid life's adventures.

10.2 Finding Sanctuary: Contentment comes from not confronting impossible life dramas.
Outer disputes can easily become inner ones, unless you sidestep others' discords altogether.

☿: Your active mind provides a quick fix or an easy escape from external problems.

♂: You tend to be actively engaged in avoiding anyone who might complicate your life.

10.3 Surrendering: The principle of aligning with personally appropriate causes.
Care is needed to be sure you are honoring your own reality and not someone else's.

⊕: A persistently moderate yet steady approach to confronting trials brings you great rewards.

☾: You tend to seek attention and approval from others, disregarding your own genuine ideals.

10.4 Exploring: Looking for great benefit and transformation in any interaction.
Being ready when opportunity knocks and appreciating what an opportunity means to you.

☊: You can hold out for the bright flash of opportunity that transforms everything.

♀: Mentally adjusting your behaviors you tailor any opening to a potential advantage.

10.5 Re-visioning: An enjoyment in confronting, often defying the commonplace.
You enjoy challenging tradition and find there are many ways to do so, lovingly or not.

♃: Your principled behavior directly challenges established tradition to question itself.

♂: Your tendency to challenge everyone and everything can attract personal reprisals.

10.6 Bringing Alignment: A personal example that is impossible for others to ignore.
Successful steps imply flourishing outcomes so long as you honor yourself and your journey.

☋: Your considered actions are often dramatically effective in their transformative outcome.

♄: If you take yourself too seriously you will miss much of the fun that life offers.

Harmony
Peace and Ideas
Harmony comes from within and emanates out to the world. Small efforts can bring about large returns.

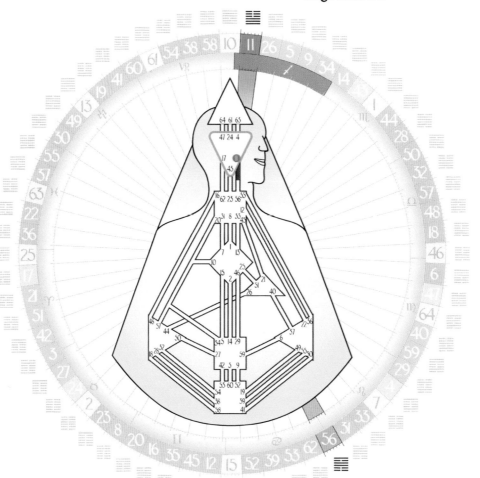

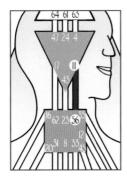

Part of Channel 11-56
The Channel of Curiosity

Center: **Mind**   Circuit: **Collective/Sensing**

Astrological Period: **Sagitarius**

Astrological Positions:

22°37'30" ♐ – 28°15'00" ♐

1:	22°37'30" ♐ – 23°33'45" ♐
2:	23°33'45" ♐ – 24°30'00" ♐
3:	24°30'00" ♐ – 25°26'15" ♐
4:	25°26'15" ♐ – 26°22'30" ♐
5:	26°22'30" ♐ – 27°18'45" ♐
6:	27°18'45" ♐ – 28°15'00" ♐

Balancing between espousing ideas that promote social harmony and embracing beliefs that are grounded in your present reality. The Left eye.

Obscurity

Obscured ⬦ Unrealistic : Idealism :: Light

11.1 Complimenting: Progressing by aligning with your immediate environment.
Your ideas come and go, finding right company in which to share them is important.
☾: You easily find those who will appreciate and help further your ideas.
♂: You can be overly worried sometimes that no one ever appreciates your ideas.

11.2 Being Independent: Peacefulness is protected through your alertness.
Tolerance, resolution and vision are required to maintain peace and foster your creative ideas.
♆: Your expansive imagination is constantly checking all possibilities for a harmonious life.
♂: Being confronted because you indulge your provocative ideas just to escape boredom.

11.3 Allowing for Change: Maintaining peacefulness requires relevant and fresh ideas.
You need to discern a difference between valuable ideas and those that are simply idealistic.
☋: Appreciating each moment, you acknowledge that times of peace come and go.
♀: You have a tendency to become lulled by an unrealistic attachment to harmony.

11.4 Sharing Ideals: An ability to consider and convey ideas of merit to others.
Some things are obvious, some things can be taught, and some things have to be transmitted.
☾: You have the gift of being able to teach and deliver concepts to almost anyone.
♀: You promote a sense of harmony that eventually appeals even to those who are disillusioned.
☉: You relay ideals which can only be transmitted to a select few.

11.5 The Ruler who Serves: Giving perspective through expansive ideals.
You overflow with beneficial ideas given either from a sense of service, or from your insecurity.
☾: Your sensibility for good concepts and how to relate them, benefits all aspects of humanity.
☿: You tend to broadcast your ideas regardless of the effect they have on those listening.

11.6 Being Flexible: Maintaining an inner balance as belief patterns change.
Renewal follows adversity when you adjust your beliefs according to prevailing circumstances.
♆: Embracing new beliefs allows you to maintain your sense of balance in changing times.
♃: You espouse ideas that will suit any situation, but sometimes at other people's expense.

12

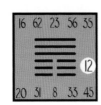

否 **Standstill**
Hindrance, Taking Stock
Being inactive in word and deed
until the moment is right to express.

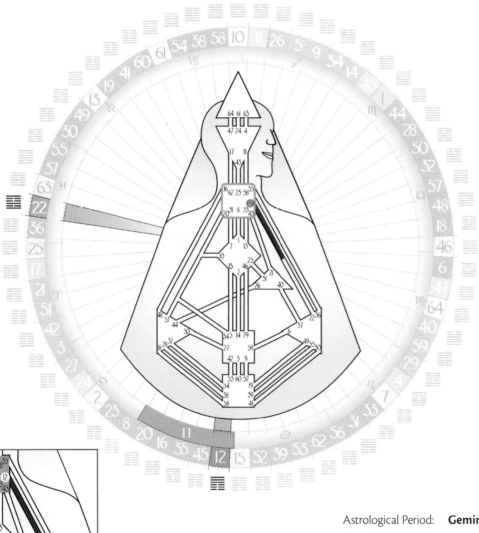

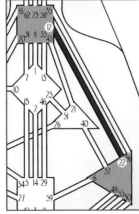

Part of Channel 12-22
The Channel of Openness

Center: **Throat** Circuit: **Individual/**
Knowing

Astrological Period: **Gemini** 〓

Astrological Positions:

22°37′30″ 〓 – 28°15′00″ 〓

1:	22°37′30″ 〓 – 23°33′45″ 〓
2:	23°33′45″ 〓 – 24°30′00″ 〓
3:	24°30′00″ 〓 – 25°26′15″ 〓
4:	25°26′15″ 〓 – 26°22′30″ 〓
5:	26°22′30″ 〓 – 27°18′45″ 〓
6:	27°18′45″ 〓 – 28°15′00″ 〓

Attuning to each moment and pausing to envision and outline prospective futures that might defy previously accepted and mainstream ways.
The Gate of Romanticism.

Vanity
Elitist ⬦ Malicious : Discrimination :: Purity

12.1 Standing Still: Appreciating how a harsh world aids your inner sense of freedom.
Withdrawing from the mainstream, you relate with those who appreciate your individual needs.
☿: By avoiding many social interactions you find harmony in your own world.
♃: You tend to qualify unreasonable isolation regardless of the effect this has on others.

12.2 Standpoint: Staying with your own truth aligns you with your own inner contentment.
Your are either disciplined in your commitments, or you lapse and become agitated waiting.
♄: Espousing natural principles you eliminate the possibility of being unbalanced by others.
☿: In restlessness you forget your natural social caution, and speak and act out of turn.

12.3 Resurging: Going beyond any past missteps allows you to move on gracefully.
Everyone makes mistakes, the greatest lesson in life is to absolve yourself and not repeat them!
♆: Attuning, through watchfulness, to the fragility we all suffer in relating with each other.
♂: A nagging sense of hopelessness that you will ever be able to have 'normal' relationships.

12.4 Prophesying: The ability to know when change is coming and the need to be ready.
Knowing the future and knowing how you will tell of it may be two very different things!
⊕: Your inner attunement with the workings of Nature can foresee and express change.
☿: You might see the future, but have trouble relating it and knowing what to do practically.

12.5 Establishing: Aligning with those aspects of your nature that are empowering.
You know 'who', 'what', and 'where' are empowering, and either utilize this gift or disregard it.
☉: You have the ability to overcome difficulties by envisioning far beyond them.
♂: You will be socially awkward as long as your emotional mix-ups remain unresolved.

12.6 Transforming: Amazing changes can come from periods of standstill.
Inventing your own rules you stand apart from the normal expressions of social behaviors.
☉: You have the means to express completely new and empowering social conditions.
⊕: Losing track of your vision and true purpose you easily get stuck in time-worn expressions.

13

同人 **The Listener**
Fellowship with Mankind
Our common purpose in these times
is in pursuing common goals, namely
expanding all possible levels and
varieties of human experience.

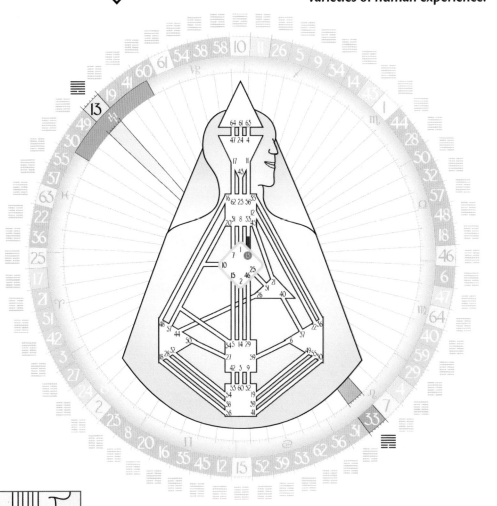

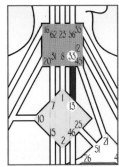

Part of Channel 13-33
The Channel of the Prodigal

Center: **Self**   Circuit: **Collective/Sensing**

Astrological Period: **Aquarius** ♒

Astrological Positions:

13°15′00″ ♒ – 18°52′30″ ♒

1:	13°15′00″ ♒ – 14°11′15″ ♒
2:	14°11′15″ ♒ – 15°07′30″ ♒
3:	15°07′30″ ♒ – 16°03′45″ ♒
4:	16°03′45″ ♒ – 17°00′00″ ♒
5:	17°00′00″ ♒ – 17°56′15″ ♒
6:	17°56′15″ ♒ – 18°52′30″ ♒

Everyone needs to experience acceptance, acknowledgement and appreciation in their journey through life. Being a magnet for those who feel disconnected and need someone to hear their story.

Discord

Naive ◇ Narrow-minded : Discernment :: Empathy

13.1 Being Open: Relating to and communing with everyone equally.
Your friendliness with others aligns the world around you.

♀: Your sensibility spreads a feeling of harmony and connectedness through everyone.

☾: You may have personal interests that disguise the intent of your expressions of concern.

13.2 Being Fair: Seeing two sides to every story and remaining unbiased.
You have the possibility of humoring, clarifying, or even being divisive in all interactions.

☾: Reflecting a moral high ground through your tolerance and consideration.

☉: Inflexibility inclines you towards being intolerant to anyone else's viewpoint or values.

13.3 Being Self-reliant: Mistrust and failure cycle through blindly taking other's guidance.
You need to find your own way after perhaps getting disillusioned with trying everyone else's!

⊕: Your naturally suspicious nature is comforted by tangible evidence. "Show me the proof!"

♀: A sense of helplessness can emerge after finding no one to trust (except yourself).

13.4 The Whisperer: The possibility of hearing life at a very deep level.
Your sensitivity to hear at great inner depth is exhausted when exposed to plain noise.

☋: Holding dearly to those who honor your nature, or actively seeking solitude in silence.

♀: Becoming exhausted in over-committing, you eventually crave times and places of solitude.

13.5 Living Symphony: Finding a purpose in, and for, everyone and everything.
You esteem, exonerate, enjoy and exalt anyone as a vital player in human experience.

♆: You have the gift to resolve all personal obstacles to attaining concord and purpose in life.

♃: You take on burdens for others when they might benefit by settling the burdens themselves.

13.6 Expounding Universal Fellowship: Seeking the best in everyone and everything, everywhere.
Apparently realistic or not, your friendliness looks for the best outcomes in everyone's life.

♂: Decisively joining with other people you expect to be able to improve their lives.

☿: You believe that by sharing your interests with others you will improve any experience.

14

大有 Prosperity
Harvesting

There is a knack to learning to embody a genuine ease in situations involving resources of property, wealth and affluence.

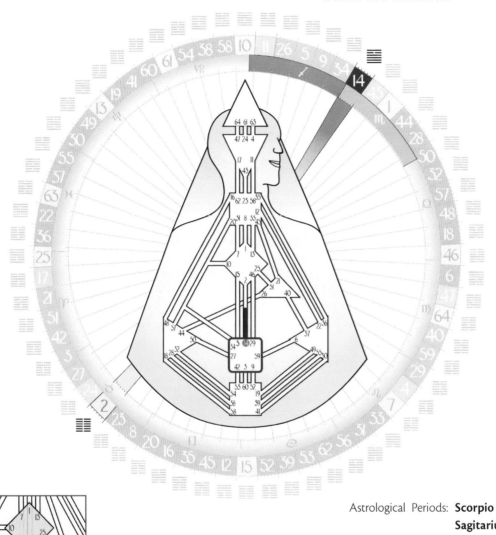

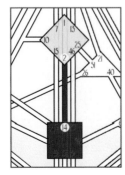

Part of Channel 2-14
The Channel of the Alchemist

Center: **Sacral** Circuit: **Individual/ Knowing**

Astrological Periods: **Scorpio** ♏
Sagitarius ♐

Astrological Positions:

24°30'00" ♏ – 00°07'30" ♐

1:	24°30'00" ♏ – 25°26'15" ♏
2:	25°26'15" ♏ – 26°22'30" ♏
3:	26°22'30" ♏ – 27°18'45" ♏
4:	27°18'45" ♏ – 28°15'00" ♏
5:	28°15'00" ♏ – 29°11'15" ♏
6:	29°11'15" ♏ – 00°07'30" ♐

The clarity of personal commitment, inner strength, detachment and perseverance, ensures great transformation and empowerment.

Compromise

Inferior ◇ Superior : Competence :: Bounteousness

14.1 Finding Satisfaction: Examining closely what it is that really motivates you.
A dependence on anything outside you to make you happy will be found to be misplaced.
♃: You have a principled approach to attaining and utilizing material resources.
☿: Attempting to control the flow of resources in life requires you to have great trust.

14.2 Engaging Wholesomeness: Growing a capability to manage all your assets elegantly.
You maximize your resources through obtaining capable assistance, or by going it alone.
♃: Your key to expanding wealth lies in receiving assistance from willing and capable helpers.
♂: If you only trust your own capability to carry everything, you will soon become overloaded.

14.3 Sacrificing: Offering your talents and resources for the good of all.
Giving for everyone's benefit (yours included), or being charitable out of a sense of obligation.
⊕: Gifting others selflessly brings you the greatest possible personal satisfaction.
♆: The delusion that holding on to extra personal resources will bring you satisfaction.

14.4 Being Secure: Personal security exists in having what you need.
You ensure your empowerment by knowing what makes you secure and having it in your life.
☾: Honing skills to ensure a personal sensation of security through any changes life brings.
♂: Exercising caution allows you to develop the personal skills you need to thrive in life.

14.5 Being Sincere: Appropriate interactions with others concerning material matters.
Your knack for handling the material world needs skills when you relate with the people in it!
☉: Your dignified ways ensures everyone's appreciation in all material interactions.
♀: Being overly friendly in material matters will inevitably lead you into misunderstandings.

14.6 Being Worthy: Existence gives resources and blessing to whomever it chooses!
A spiritual and/or material approach to the responsibilities associated with wealth.
☉: Your easy attunement to wealth gives you the humility to be generous and grateful.
⊕: A practical approach allows you to find a balance between material and spiritual realms.

15

謙

Humanity
Humanity, Extremes
You find your role in all possible extremes and conditions that life offers.

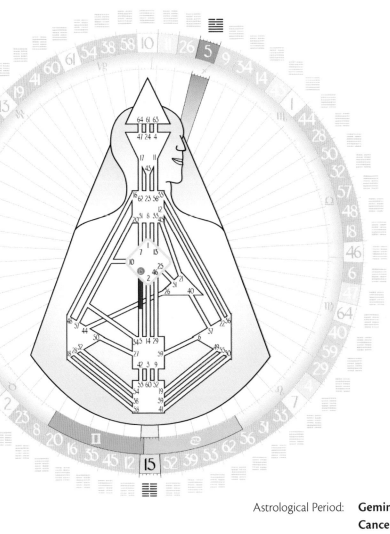

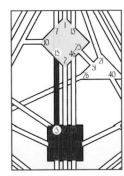

Part of Channel 5-15
The Channel of Rhythm

Center: **Self**   Circuit: **Collective/Logic**

Astrological Period: **Gemini** ♊
                       Cancer ♋

Astrological Positions:

28°15'00" ♊ – 03°52'30"

1:	28°15'00" ♊ – 29°11'15" ♊
2:	29°11'15" ♊ – 00°07'30"
3:	00°07'30" – 01°03'45"
4:	01°03'45" – 02°00'00"
5:	02°00'00" – 02°56'15"
6:	02°56'15" – 03°52'30"

Having friends and acquaintances in all levels of society, implies you might have a difficulty being attached to, or be controlled by anyone in particular.
(Gate 15 is common to every life form.)

Dullness
Empty ⬦ Extremist : Magnetism :: Florescence

15.1 Having Humility: Having the self-discipline to transcend all manner of life issues.
You either maintain a sensibility to your nature and needs, or an insecurity that is immodest.

♀: Honoring the harmony in any relationship allows you to facilitate any enterprise.

♂: Rushing to enact and pronounce your personal achievements can alienate others.

15.2 Being Persistent: Finding reassurance by maintaining your sincerity and integrity.
Your moderation as well as your extreme conduct, has a profound effect on others.

☉: You have the strength to accept your own particular ways as natural in the flow of life.

⊕: Contriving outcomes by comparing your extreme ways to other peoples' moderate ones.

15.3 Being Modest: An unwavering commitment to finish what you start.
Accomplishing deeds without asserting your supremacy affects the quality of your whole life.

⊕: Completing all tasks while you remain unassuming in achievement.

☿: The possibility you communicate a personal superiority of yourself over other people and their ways.

15.4 Centering: Restraining any extremes in your life that do not reflect love.
Being loving and true to the flow of life requires you to constantly check your inner guidance.

♃: The humility to achieve your best in a way that is in accord with your highest ideals.

♄: A dogmatic approach to going your own way that awkwardly strives for goals.

15.5 Fellowship: Attuning to the needs of all those in extreme positions.
You guide those with less experience through tough situations, by virtue, or by being brash.

♃: Your leadership quality can handle the turbulent flow of life and also maintain humility.

☊: Any push to impose on those less competent than yourself will end up alienating them.

15.6 Commentary: Setting an example by taking responsibility for your own circumstances in life.
By accepting and appreciating who you are, you find an exemplary course through life.

☊: You can take charge and steer any situation at any time, and do so with humility.

♀: Seeking harmony in all interactions you can blame others when things appear to go wrong!

16

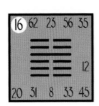

豫 Selectivity
Enthusiasm and Skills
You have the ability in sorting through all manner of potential endeavors and processes to identify those that actually have relevance, usefulness and a prospective future.

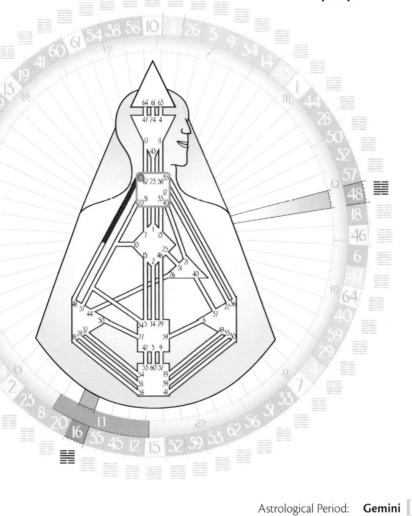

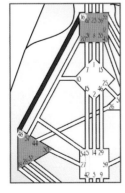

Part of Channel 16-48
The Channel of Talent

Center: **Throat**   Circuit: **Collective/Logic**

Astrological Period: **Gemini** ♊

Astrological Positions:

05°45'00" ♊ – 11°22'30" ♊

1:	05°45'00" ♊ – 06°41'15" ♊
2:	06°41'15" ♊ – 07°37'30" ♊
3:	07°37'30" ♊ – 08°33'45" ♊
4:	08°33'45" ♊ – 09°30'00" ♊
5:	09°30'00" ♊ – 10°26'15" ♊
6:	10°26'15" ♊ – 11°22'30" ♊

When everything is in a state of preparation, it is possible to relax, sometimes to harness more skills.

Indifference

Misidentified $\diamondsuit$ Scattered : Versatility :: Mastery

16.1 Paying attention: Enthusiasm can be aligned to the real needs of the moment or not.
Having a clear grasp of what is confronting you requires presence, interest and detachment.
$\oplus$: You can easily get involved in situations without always considering what's really going on.
$\underline{\varphi}$: You tend to make declarations on behalf of other people that cannot easily be substantiated.

16.2 Being Watchful: You consider life objectively and comment accordingly.
You have the ability to see through to the merits of any scheme both neutrally and critically.
$\odot$: You have natural skill to judge any situation impartially, regardless of what others say.
$\underline{\varphi}$: You express a pointed analysis that might easily dampen other people's excitement.

16.3 Re-forming: Delight comes in winning your own accomplishments.
There is a fine line between needing encouragement from outside and going it alone.
$\mathbb{C}$: Attuning to your own enthusiasm you gauge how to propel your life through any situation.
$\male$: The need to have others aim, confirm and sometimes bankroll your skills or talents.

16.4 Guiding: Confidence in dealing with life's problems draws others to your side.
It's easy for you to give support and recognition to others, or you might ignore their offerings.
$\jupiter$: Your enthusiasm for combining efforts aimed at lofty goals will gather widespread support.
$\male$: In pushing to get ahead you can fail to acknowledge any assistance you get, or need for it.

16.5 Resisting: An unwillingness to encourage yourself or others to move on in life.
You recognize potentials, but tend to avoid endorsing them if you consider them unattainable.
ω: You are rarely overtly enthusiastic about anything or anyone, before seeing real results.
$\mathbb{C}$: Moodiness will result in your being reluctant to encourage advancing any schemes.

16.6 Re-assessing: Objective evaluation of realistic goals.
You either see things as they really are, or get flustered by others' expectations and lose clarity.
ψ: By envisioning everyone's views, you adjust your goals accordingly, practically or not.
$\jupiter$: Expanding any concept regardless of outcomes, you'll eventually become disenchanted.

17

隨 Following
Opinions
Debate and discussion temper all opinions to a point where they stand as a base for concepts and ideals aligned with the potential future wellbeing of everyone.

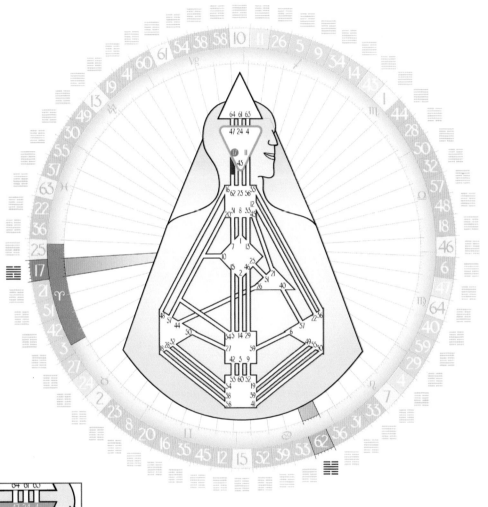

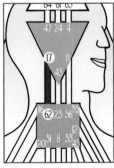

Part of Channel 17-62

The Channel of the Organizer

Center: **Mind**   Circuit: **Collective/Logic**

Astrological Period: **Aries** ♈

Astrological Positions:

03°52'30" ♈ – 09°30'00" ♈

1:	03°52'30" ♈ –	04°48'15" ♈
2:	04°48'45" ♈ –	05°45'30" ♈
3:	05°45'00" ♈ –	06°41'45" ♈
4:	06°41'15" ♈ –	07°37'00" ♈
5:	07°37'30" ♈ –	08°33'15" ♈
6:	08°33'45" ♈ –	09°30'00" ♈

Following trains of thought to find a logical balance within the many
perspectives of what life is, or could be, all about. The Right eye.
(Gate 17 is a transpecial bridge that attunes with mammals.)

Opinion
Opinionless ◇ Opinionated : Far-sightedness :: Omniscience

17.1 Being Open-minded: Recognizing the potential dualities in all things.
You appreciate many different views of life, none of which by themselves, are right or wrong.

♂: You promote many different opinions while still holding true to your internal principles.

♀: Losing sight of your principles when your sense of harmony is disturbed by others' opinions.

17.2 Assessing: Preferring company that moves you to a higher appreciation of life.
You find meaning for yourself by relating with others, whether your relationships last or not.

☉: You develop your qualitative opinions through your attention to all of life's interactions.

☾: A moodiness can cause you to value your opinions over your friendships.

17.3 Selecting: Appreciating the best influences for inner growth.
You either foster viewpoints that bring maturity, or endorse ones without lasting significance.

⊙: You have an enduring and transformative effect when aligned with honorable company.

⊕: Your tendency to seek any means to obtain results will cause you to miss essential issues.

17.4 Being Unselfish: Open to finding the best measures to further everyone.
Opinions can conceal ulterior motives giving you the opportunity to test your inner principles.

⊙: You have a transformative effect on others when your motives and principles are aligned.

♃: You express opinions that attract everyone even those people you would rather avoid.

17.5 Interconnecting: The recognition that 'We are One.'
You attain your highest aims by your virtue, or by attempting to disregard cosmic coincidence.

☊: Your inventiveness is aligned with spiritual and/or worldly resolutions.

♂: Your push for personal recognition can rule out receiving assistance from any other source.

17.6 Being The Bodhisattva: Attuning to the higher levels of human consciousness.
You foster and express wisdom in ways to honor and align others in their own lives.

☾: "The finger pointing at the moon." You can access the sincerity and simplicity of life

♃: By attaining to a human comprehension of Existence you are a teacher of teachers.

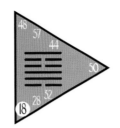

蠱 Improving
Finding Remedy.
(Work on what has been spoiled)
All traditions and customs need
constant review to find if they are
presently wholesome and healthy.

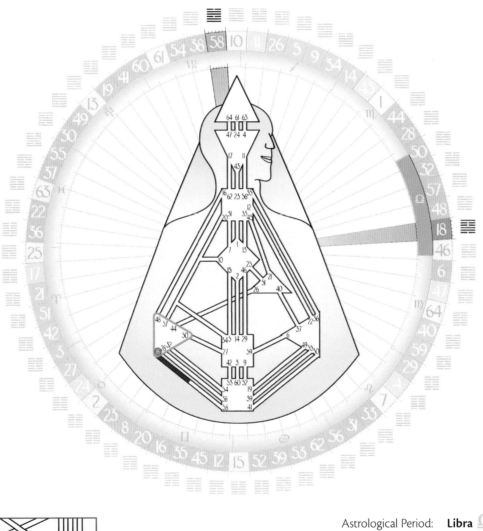

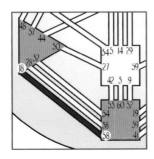

Part of Channel 18-58
The Channel of Judgement
Center: **Spleen**   Circuit: **Collective/Logic**

Astrological Period: **Libra** ♎
Astrological Positions:
    03°52′30″ ♎ – 09°30′00″ ♎

1:   03°52′30″ ♎ – 04°48′15″ ♎
2:   04°48′45″ ♎ – 05°45′30″ ♎
3:   05°45′00″ ♎ – 06°41′45″ ♎
4:   06°41′15″ ♎ – 07°37′00″ ♎
5:   07°37′30″ ♎ – 08°33′15″ ♎
6:   08°33′45″ ♎ – 09°30′00″ ♎

Dispassionately re-evaluating unbalanced systems, interactions, practices and procedures aims humanity to grow towards a flourishing future. Perfectionism can border on neurosis.

Judgment

Conforming ◇ Judgmental : Integrity :: Perfecting

18.1 Being Paternalistic: The difficulties involved in updating male traditions.
Patriarchal traditions are rooted in his-tory and you examine them to find present relevance.
⊕: You have the endurance to gradually bring practical modifications to ancient judgments.
♃: By expounding life from traditional views you will remain stuck in someone else's past.

18.2 Honoring the Goddess: Instilled fears involving the power of the feminine.
Any tendency to suppress the feminine side of your nature requires great inner watchfulness.
☋: You have the potential to transform your inherited fears through diligence and alertness.
☽: Sensitive to those who instilled your fears you are reluctant to hurt their feelings.

18.3 Being Impetuous: Driven to break with the past and get to the future, now!
Examining what is no longer needed in your life gives you the possibility to be free from it!
♆: Highly critical of your old conditioning you find imaginative ways to address it.
♃: Any attempts to bypass or discount your conditioning eventually brings you remorse.

18.4 Allowing things to be: Attempting to cure symptoms and not causes.
Going to the heart of problematic issues you see if you actually attract them. A call to meditate.
⊕: Fixating on curing your apparent inabilities, or finding freedom in your own clarity.
☿: Mental anxiety and procrastination are brought on when you indulge others' criticism.

18.5 Self-correcting: An honesty to resolve conditioning through being alert.
Your watchfulness and presence in all situations can clarify any conditioning and bring relief.
♄: Any improvements are sustained through relationships that relax your fears of worthiness.
☊: Relating to others in ways that do not resolve conditioning, you cause further imbalance.

18.6 Being the Buddha: Going beyond all conditioning.
You dedicate yourself to universal concerns and spiritual development for all beings.
♂: You have the ability and drive to expound universal truths wherever you are.
☽: You exude the reassurance to reveal that there are no insurmountable problems in life.

19

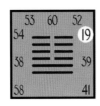

臨 **Approach**
The need to find inclusion
Reaching out to find how life connects
us all and an urge to end separation
and re-establish unity.

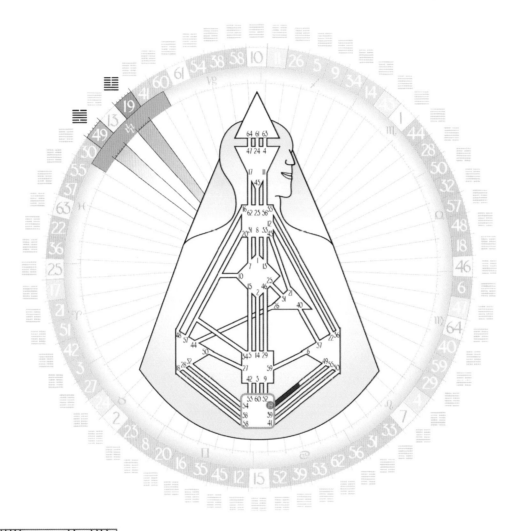

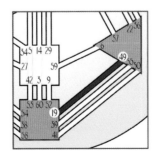

Part of Channel 19-49
The Channel of Sensitivity

Center: **Root**   Circuit: **Tribal/Community**

Astrological Period: **Aquarius** ♒

Astrological Positions:

07°37′30″ ♒ – 13°15′00″ ♒

1:   07°37′30″ ♒ – 08°33′45″ ♒
2:   08°33′45″ ♒ – 09°30′00″ ♒
3:   09°30′00″ ♒ – 10°26′15″ ♒
4:   10°26′15″ ♒ – 11°22′30″ ♒
5:   11°22′30″ ♒ – 12°18′45″ ♒
6:   12°18′45″ ♒ – 13°15′00″ ♒

Sensing others' needs often more than they do themselves.
An internal energy drives you to make contact to establish a starting
point to realization. Flirtation draws attention.
Co-Dependence
Needy ⬦ Isolated : Sensitivity :: Sacrifice

19.1 Finding Mutuality: Reaching out to find supportive company.
Your emotional detachment and inner equilibrium are tested through interactions with others.
⊙: You have the strength to hold to your principles when confronted by outside influences.
☾: A tendency when considering others' needs to get distracted from your own.

19.2 Cooperating: A right approach wins allies.
You have a natural gift to assist others by summoning support from many sources.
♃: You overcome all difficulties by trusting in your uncontrived high ideals.
☿: "Being there" for others so that you feel included and not necessarily always to assist them.

19.3 Getting Involved: Great care is needed to distinguish real needs and wants.
Relationships yield poor attitudes if you are motivated by neediness instead of inner clarity.
♀: You maintain a natural inner harmony in your approval of, and by others.
☾: Your moodiness can become a neediness that dominates all your interactions with others.

19.4 Maturing: Composed behavior in group interactions furthers teamwork.
You are mostly at ease being among others and help to combine everyone's contributions.
♂: You drive others to excel through your efforts, example and encouragement.
♀: Within a group you tend to be promoting harmony rather than results.

19.5 Delegating: Offering up personal initiatives to capable helpers.
You support everyone by delegating to capable assistants while retaining overall responsibility.
⊕: Your inner confidence and strength of purpose enjoys seeing your associates get ahead.
♃: When you delegate authority without regard to someone's capabilities, chaos ensues!

19.6 The Sage: Teaching about inner growth from your own depth of experience.
You can provide immense support to others through imparting compassionate wisdom.
♃: Your magnanimous nature must sometimes be enticed from you to engage with others.
♂: You prefer to be approached respectfully, so that you can more easily impart your wisdom.

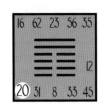

觀 The "Now"
Contemplation: Watching
The Gateway to knowing is simple:
Be in the Here and Now!

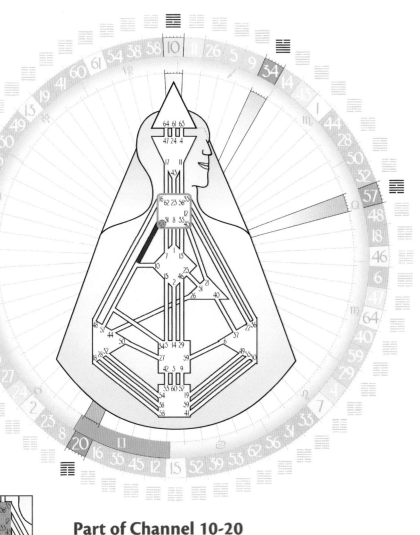

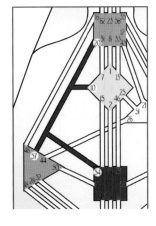

Part of Channel 10-20
The Channel of Awakening

Part of Channel 20-34
The Channel of Keeping Busy

Part of Channel 20-57
The Channel of Involuntary Impulses

Center: **Throat**   Circuit: **Individual/
Integration/Knowing**

Astrological Period: **Gemini** ⬚

Astrological Positions:

	00°07′30″ Ⅱ – 05°45′00″ Ⅱ		
1:	00°07′30″ Ⅱ – 01°03′45″ Ⅱ		
2:	01°03′45″ Ⅱ – 02°00′00″ Ⅱ		
3:	02°00′00″ Ⅱ – 02°56′15″ Ⅱ		
4:	02°56′15″ Ⅱ – 03°52′30″ Ⅱ		
5:	03°52′30″ Ⅱ – 04°48′45″ Ⅱ		
6:	04°48′45″ Ⅱ – 05°45′00″ Ⅱ		

By sitting in the Gateway between "this" and "that," and watching every aspect of life dispassionately you are led to find clarity in your life. Concentration leads to Contemplation leads to Meditation.

Superficiality

Worried ⬦ Vacant : Self Assurance : : Presence

20.1 Simplicity. . . . . . is the key to awareness!
Each small event is a part of a larger scheme of events. Your own viewing of life is essential.

♀: You find beauty and harmony in apparent simplicity. For example : A panoramic view.

☾: A moody oversimplification of life can cause you to shirk personal responsibility.

20.2 Viewpoint: Weighing personal perspectives with the reality of the World.
If your unaffected observations are not appreciated, you can easily become discouraged.

♀: Broadening your perspectives through finding harmony in every moment.

☾: If you take everything seriously you'll form narrow and potentially moody viewpoints.

20.3 Being Objective: Developing an ability to watch thoughts and actions impassively.
Establishing guidelines by dispassionately watching the effect you have on your world.

☉: Honoring your 'witnessing consciousness' you'll find assists you to glide through your life.

⊕: Your self-consciousness can be a stumbling block when you are relating in the world.

20.4 Observing: Promoting the best influences in your world.
Impacting situations by recognizing and enabling the best attributes in yourself and others.

♃: You expound knowledge in varied ways according to the requirements of the moment.

☿: You communicate through remarks that may or may not have any instant practical value.

20.5 Meditating: Watching your deepest thoughts and feelings dispassionately.
Open to hearing the world's comments on your life, you engage from a place of inner clarity.

♄: You have a disciplined approach towards promoting sound standards in the world.

☊: Becoming unhappy with your present reality you tend to chase drama and diversion.

20.6 Reflecting: Considering those agendas that benefit everyone.
Your detached presence amasses realistic knowledge that is available for everyone to utilize.

♀: You have the ability to expound your individual clarity for the greater good.

☿: Your ability to communicate promotes knowledge of all kinds whether it's useful or not.

21

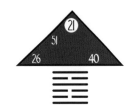

噬嗑 **Control**

The Hunter

The expression of willpower employs strategies to take charge on the material level.

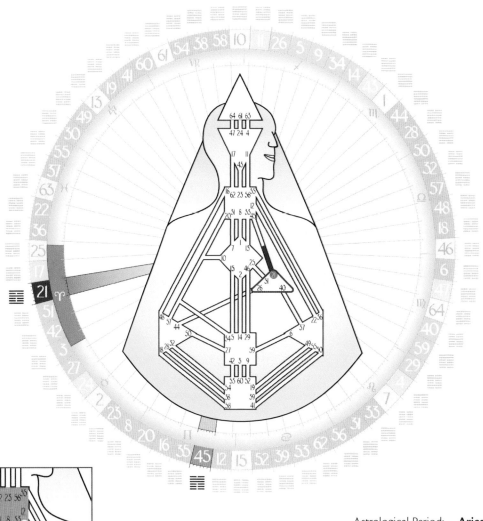

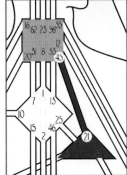

Part of Channel 21-45

The Channel of Money

Center: **Heart** Circuit: **Tribal/ Entrepreneurial**

Astrological Period: **Aries** ♈

Astrological Positions:

09°30'00" ♈ – 15°07'30" ♈

1:	09°30'00" ♈ – 10°26'15" ♈
2:	10°26'15" ♈ – 11°22'30" ♈
3:	11°22'30" ♈ – 12°18'45" ♈
4:	12°18'45" ♈ – 13°15'00" ♈
5:	13°15'00" ♈ – 14°11'15" ♈
6:	14°11'15" ♈ – 15°07'30" ♈

By "getting to the heart of matters," willfulness is employed with consideration for the common good, or if ego is applied, towards exclusively personal advantage. The Hunter/Huntress engages with his/her quarry.

Control

Being controlled ◇ Controlling : Authority :: Valor

21.1 Being Responsible: Correcting your small mistakes allows for easy growth in life.
Your mistakes are natural but need correcting responsibly to avoid having problems later.
♂: You derive respect without needing to be tough on yourself or others.
☾: Indulging a lack of will power and "giving up" continually diminishes your convictions.

21.2 Courage: Giving and receiving correction for any necessary reforms.
Your willingness to improve life standards often requires strong, yet virtuous remedies.
♂: Deliberately applying correction for yourself and others when handling irresponsible acts.
♆: Any reluctance to achieve reforms certainly results in losing your sense of responsibility.

21.3 Hesitating: Being potentially overwhelmed by apparent circumstances.
Getting caught up in other people's ego issues always affects your level of commitment in life.
♆: You will suffer at the hands of those "in power," unless you follow your own material path.
♃: You tend to needlessly go-it-alone at the expense of your own well-being.

21.4 "Biting the bullet": Dealing with all situations in life using great self-control.
You easily establish your authority by weighing up any environment and the people in it.
♃: You expand into material success through strategic moves and not by conditioned reflex.
⊕: Continually establishing your separateness easily distracts you from your real needs.

21.5 Being Gallant: Considering who merits efforts to bring the best reforms.
Using your willpower actively or by delegating, you keep control and direct material matters.
♃: You easily apply your willful authority for the ultimate benefit of everyone.
⊙: Insisting on your way, regardless of consequences, you will eventually become alienated.

21.6 Amending: A delicate touch can bring needed adjustments to any situation.
Being available to implement necessary controls or losing focus and promoting confusion.
⊙: Displaying your willpower in any situation you will automatically bring about changes.
♀: Promoting harmony at any cost rather than facing facts, you can expect disorder in your life.

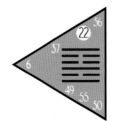

22

賁 **Grace**
Adorning: Favor
In the world, the emotional energy
of Grace enriches life through
beauty,
adorning and affection.

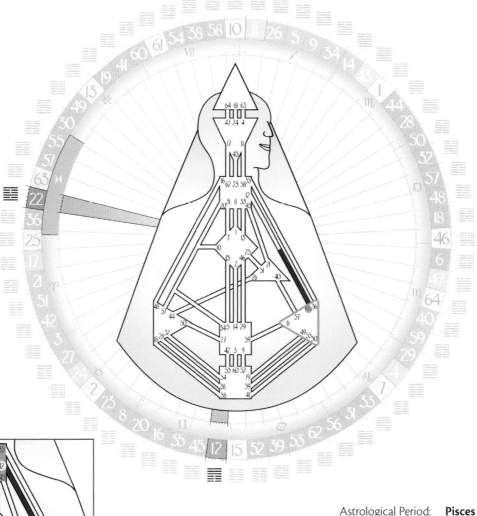

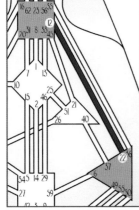

Part of Channel 12-22
The Channel of Openness

Center: **Emotions**   Circuit: **Individual/**
Knowing

Astrological Period: **Pisces** ♓

Astrological Positions:

	17°00′00″ ♓ – 22°37′30″ ♓
1:	17°00′00″ ♓ – 17°56′15″ ♓
2:	17°56′15″ ♓ – 18°52′30″ ♓
3:	18°52′30″ ♓ – 19°48′45″ ♓
4:	19°48′45″ ♓ – 20°45′00″ ♓
5:	20°45′00″ ♓ – 21°41′15″ ♓
6:	21°41′15″ ♓ – 22°37′30″ ♓

On the Spiritual level, Grace is the blessing that comes through clear emotional alignment with Consciousness. When challenged emotionally Grace can sometimes become dis-Grace.
(Gate 22 is a transpecial bridge that attunes with mammals.)

Dishonor
Proper ◇ Inappropriate : Graciousness :: Grace

22.1 Being Gracious: Assuming humility and appreciation for all aspects of life.
Relying on your own essential worth and being open to embrace any roles offered by life.

☾: The emotional awareness to feel empowered and guided from within your core.

♂: Assuming roles which are not actually required or relevant, inevitably brings you problems.

22.2 Charming: The natural ability to embellish and adorn.
Beauty and style are attributes you use to promote enchantment, fascination and distraction.

☉: Your natural emotional style attracts others, and moves and uplifts their lives.

♃: If you place style before emotional awareness in your life you will eventually promote fallout.

22.3 Enchanting: Grace in Perfection. A charmed life. Good fortune.
You embody Grace as all things wondrous, aligning yourself with simple Universal truths.

♄: You align emotional energy and a perception that empowers your inner radiance.

♂: Your pure physicality embodies grace in all your movements and activities.

22.4 Impressing: Empowering all interactions by aligning to their requirements.
Your inner radiance and external brilliance transforms the quality of all interactions.

♆: You have a very particular way to interact that rejects many formalities adopted by others.

♂: You may find yourself manipulating circumstances in an attempt to force interactions.

22.5 Inner Beauty: Remembering the importance of your own true nature.
Being true to yourself even as your grace and inner light is perceived in many ways by others.

♃: You have the individual's strength to empower emotional clarity in any social interaction.

♂: The possibility of being misunderstood for your distinctive stance in social situations.

22.6 Being Sophisticated: Simple elegance is one of your highest attributes.
Your inner brightness exudes grace through calm sincerity and objectivity in any situation.

☉: Your serene presence easily allows you to take charge in emotionally volatile situations.

♂: Your inner brilliance will always be perceived as unique and provocative.

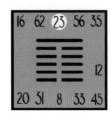

 剝 **Assimilation**
Stabilizing
Peeling away the "non-essential"
reveals what is substantial.

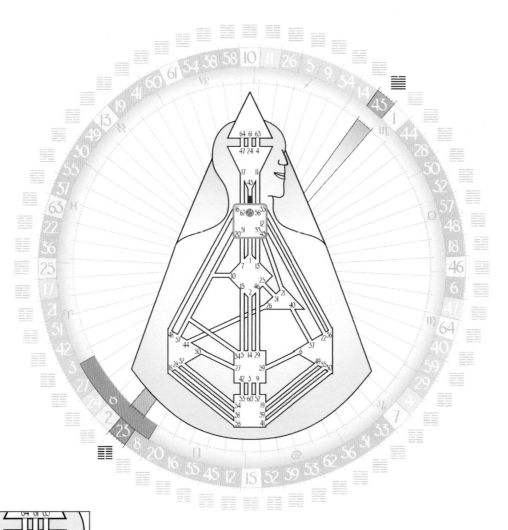

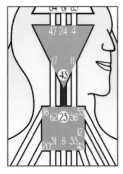

Part of Channel 23-43
The Channel of Structuring

Center: **Throat**   Circuit: **Individual/ Knowing**

Astrological Period: **Taurus** ♉

Astrological Positions:

	18°52'30" ♉ – 24°30'00" ♉
1:	18°52'30" ♉ – 19°48'15" ♉
2:	19°48'45" ♉ – 20°45'30" ♉
3:	20°45'00" ♉ – 21°41'45" ♉
4:	21°41'15" ♉ – 22°37'00" ♉
5:	22°37'30" ♉ – 23°33'15" ♉
6:	23°33'45" ♉ – 24°30'00" ♉

Standing up for your truth in the face of adversity, or stepping away from your straightforward path and considering yourself obliged to take some kind of action. The great need for speech skills.

Complexity
Dumb ◇ Fragmented : Simplicity :: Quintessence

23.1 Validating: Aiming your attention on what really needs attention.
You strive to find the inner conviction to continue relating to life's changing circumstances.

♃: You express personal insights that may or may not represent the truth of the moment.

♂: By expressing your personal views you will often provoke disruptive reactions in others.

23.2 Tolerating: Naturally relating to circumstances from a personal resolve.
Being self-righteous or detached does not necessarily help you express yourself clearly.

♃: The gift of the gab, to talk your way into and through all manner of life's obstacles.

☾: Being argumentative can become a way of life but ultimately will not serve you.

23.3 Expressing Uniqueness: Trusting in yourself while being committed to others.
Staying true to your own ways but also noticing how what other people do and say affects you.

☉: Expressing your individuality while diligently holding to your personal truth.

☊: You speak in a way that your expressions can attract concerns, suspicion and retributions.

23.4 Diversifying: Individual strength overcomes all tribulations.
Your individual, impulsive expressions often confound generally accepted ways of life.

☉: The effect of the things you say requires you to question what it is you hear yourself say.

⊕: Expressing your insights freely inevitably results in your isolation from the mainstream.

23.5 Acquiescing: The mutual benefit in offering differing, even contrary choices.
You, the individual, have the means to interact with others for personal or mutual advantage.

♃: You have the gift of being able to relate your personal insights for everyone's gain.

☾: You can be driven by a need to cooperate for personal ease rather than mutual benefits.

23.6 Synthesizing: Creating new forms by combining many different possibilities.
Remaining neutral while under pressure from the status quo allows you to propose new visions.

♂: Your individual way empowers the possibility of directing diverse options towards a unity.

♃: Your expansive nature tends to prefer and encourage diversity to unity.

24

復 Returning
Rationalizing
What goes around in the Mind comes around in the Mind, until cycles become spirals and innovation and transformation happen.

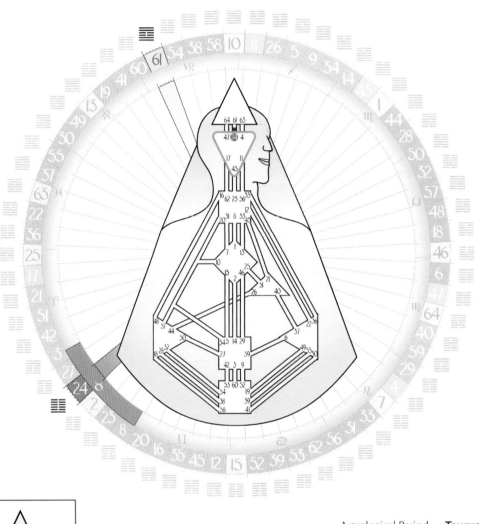

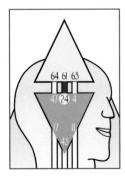

Part of Channel 24-61
The Channel of the Thinker

Center: **Mind**   Circuit: **Individual/Knowing**

Astrological Period: **Taurus** ♉

Astrological Positions:

07°37'30" ♉ – 13°15'00" ♉

1: 07°37'30" ♉ – 08°33'45" ♉
2: 08°33'45" ♉ – 09°30'00" ♉
3: 09°30'00" ♉ – 10°26'15" ♉
4: 10°26'15" ♉ – 11°22'30" ♉
5: 11°22'30" ♉ – 12°18'45" ♉
6: 12°18'45" ♉ – 13°15'00" ♉

By cycling through refined solutions you come to know the limitations of rational thought. Truth is experienced in silence.

Addiction

Frozen ◇ Addictive : Invention :: Silence

24.1 Being Principled: A constant need to review what is personally meaningful.
Your mental processes can excuse you from living your own truth for one rationale or another.
☉: You have the clear intent to proceed in life while aligning firmly with your principles.
♆: You reassess obscure thoughts while justifying inaction and lack of conviction.

24.2 Renewing: Attracting a loving environment while under duress.
All adversity brings growth when you remember who and what truly aids and inspires you.
☾: You are constantly re-attuning to empowering, evolving concepts that bring benefits.
♂: You easily isolate yourself from common concerns as though you are all alone.

24.3 Being Indecisive: Trying to think your way through life.
A reliance on old, rotating mental concepts can bring you successes but no lasting satisfaction.
♀: By softening your mental attitudes you can to be open to other means of being guided.
♃: You vacillate between many possibilities without conclusions. The thinka-/worka-holic.

24.4 Being Attentive: Cultivating mental clarity while in the company of others.
You need to look for the balance between an easy mental pattern and a personally correct one.
♄: Your disciplined review includes all options and continuously realigns them with personal truth.
♆: A dreamy nature promotes fantasy realms rather than allowing you to face your reality.

24.5 Returning: The resolution to renounce false trails and resume invention.
Through clarity and determination you make a clean break with the past, and start afresh.
☾: Empowering new inspirations is possible when you terminate stale ones.
♂: A rigid rationalization of old concepts blocks any chance for you to be refreshed.

24.6 Relenting: Dropping old concepts in the face of life's new offerings.
Past missteps need not limit the range of new choices if you revisit your own clear Authority.
♃: Your relaxed and rational thought process recognizes and welcomes all of life's gifts.
☊: Obstinacy can cause irrational worries that hinder personal development.

25

无妄 **Innocence**
The Unsuspecting
Innocence is our natural
state, unattached to
consequence......
It is inherent trust, honesty,
and sincerity.

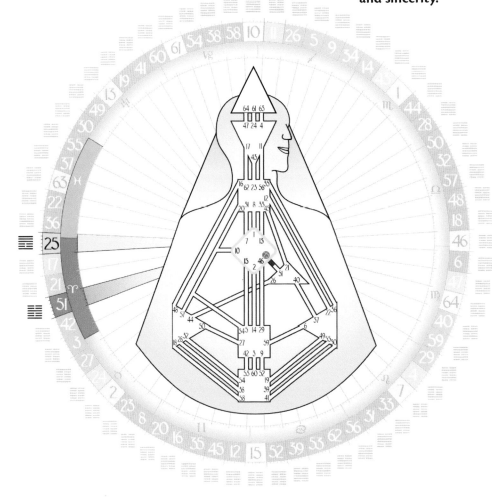

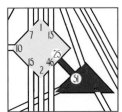

Part of Channel 25-51

The Channel of Initiation

Center: **Self**   Circuit: **Individual/
                                 Centering**

Astrological Period: **Pisces** ♓
                        Aries ♈

Astrological Positions:

	28°15′00″ ♓ – 03°52′30″ ♈
1:	28°15′00″ ♓ – 29°11′15″ ♓
2:	29°11′15″ ♓ – 00°07′30″ ♈
3:	00°07′30″ ♈ – 01°03′45″ ♈
4:	01°03′45″ ♈ – 02°00′00″ ♈
5:	02°00′00″ ♈ – 02°56′15″ ♈
6:	02°56′15″ ♈ – 03°52′30″ ♈

Universal Love emanates from an unaffected and free nature that takes nothing for granted.

Constriction

Ignorant ⬦ Cold : Acceptance :: Universal Love

25.1 Loving: Living without ulterior motives

Your heartfelt spontaneity is potentially prone to being disturbed by outside influences.

♆: A deep attunement and interplay with the mysterious courses your life takes.

☿: An inner insecurity inclines you to express yourself out of a need to compare.

25.2 Being Present: All expectations divert appreciation from the Now.

You either live freely for the moment or try anticipating results and remain unfulfilled.

☿: You have an aptitude to stay present to each moment, living innocently and in freedom.

♂: Pushing to realize dreams you lose your delight in life when outcomes are disappointing.

25.3 Adjusting: Accepting unexpected events with equanimity.

When things appear to go wrong you either accept the results or feel forsaken and hopeless.

♂: The power to remain unruffled in times of loss by persevering in your innocent love of life.

☉: You have a potential for personal devastation in your life when shocked by, or handed loss.

25.4 Being Blameless: True innocence cannot be tainted.

When aligning with inner vision, your innocent stance is unperturbed by any disturbances.

♀: The Spiritual Warrior who strides through life unscathed by all trials and disasters.

♃: Maintaining the highest ideals even when no one else cares.

25.5 Healthiness: There is no worldly cure for Spiritual sickness.

By guarding your health through right associations and attitudes you can greatly assist others.

♀: The healer who calls on the power of Spirit to heal and be healed.

♃: Misjudging your Spirit nature can induce you to constantly overextend yourself.

25.6 Misunderstanding: Adhering to knowledge will undermine true innocence.

Ultimately, knowledge rarely serves you, especially when you try second-guessing Existence.

⊕: You remain steadfast in your pursuit of purity even if you have to reinvent yourself.

☊: Brilliantly different though you may be, knowledge alone seldom brings you contentment.

26

大畜 **Accumulation**
Fortitude
This direct nature harnesses
willpower and commits to
great accomplishments and
substantial material rewards.

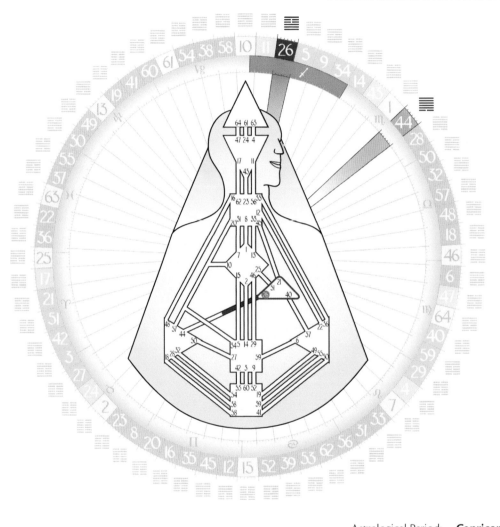

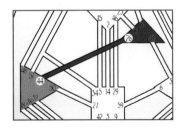

Part of Channel 26-44
The Channel of Enterprise

Center: **Heart**   Circuit: **Tribal/
Entrepreneurial**

Astrological Period: **Capricorn** ♐

Astrological Positions:

17°00'00" ♐ – 22°37'30" ♐

1:	17°00'00" ♐ – 17°56'15" ♐
2:	17°56'15" ♐ – 18°52'30" ♐
3:	18°52'30" ♐ – 19°48'45" ♐
4:	19°48'45" ♐ – 20°45'00" ♐
5:	20°45'00" ♐ – 21°41'15" ♐
6:	21°41'15" ♐ – 22°37'30" ♐

There exists an internal balance between fulfilling your own
and others' needs.
(Gate 26 connects into the instinctual realm of birds, reptiles and fish.)
Pride
Manipulative (Covertly) ⬦ Boastful : Artfulness :: Invisibility

26

26.1 Pausing: Waiting patiently for the right time to act.
Sometimes you cannot move any further in life without attracting and collecting problems.
Ψ: You use your lively imagination to resolve dilemmas and thus avoid reckless actions.
♂: Insisting on being separate you force yourself into many activities that cause disruptions.

26.2 Being Self-restrained: Patience is a virtue that serves in the long term.
When held up by forces beyond your control you are best advised to exercise patience.
☉: You exercise your power by progressively accumulating experience and resources.
☋: Forcing the pace and overriding past experiences, your path through life can be costly.

26.3 Being Prepared: Being clear in your motivations and how to exercise them well.
You succeed with or without the help of others when you overcome your fears and doubts.
☉: Your strength of will to align with your goals allows you to gather support to attain them.
♄: You succumb to obstacles and challenges if you ignore what people around you really want.

26.4 Preventing: Keeping away from irrelevant and dishonorable forms of interactions.
You uphold what you deem is honorably right or implement some questionable standards.
☋: The strength of your willpower transforms even the most rigid and obdurate situations.
♄: You implement techniques that support bending 'the rules' to get your own way.

26.5 Harnessing: Utilizing your accumulated energies wisely.
Your willful energy requires careful managing or it will continuously bring you confrontations.
♂: Directing your accumulated energy carefully gives you the potential to attract rewards.
♀: You prefer to maintain a comfortable stance rather than relate to real circumstances.

26.6 Being Poised: Creative energy is released from a place of inner equilibrium.
Accumulating and utilizing energy wisely needs you to be balanced : this balance is internal.
☉: Your willful actions are always going to be justified by their lasting appropriateness.
☾: You might notice that your moodiness is more symbolic than real.

27

頤 **Nourishing**
Nurturing
Caring qualifies the needs of health
and well-being in all aspects of life.

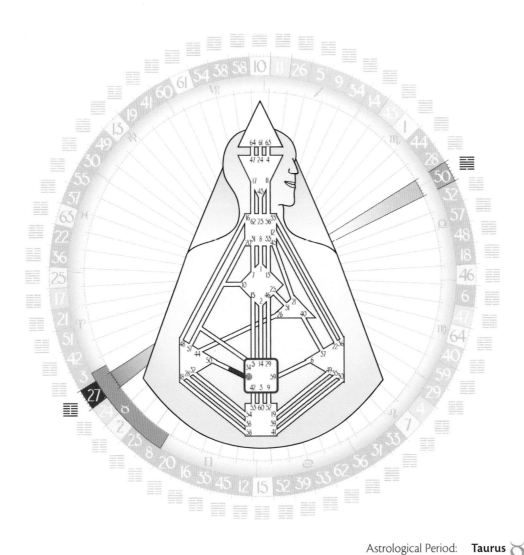

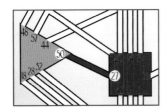

Part of Channel 27-50
The Channel of Preservation

Center: **Sacral**   Circuit: **Tribal/Defense**

Astrological Period: **Taurus** ♉

Astrological Positions:

02°00'00" ♉ – 07°37'30" ♉

1:	02°00'00" ♉ – 02°56'15" ♉
2:	02°56'15" ♉ – 03°52'30" ♉
3:	03°52'30" ♉ – 04°48'45" ♉
4:	04°48'45" ♉ – 05°45'00" ♉
5:	05°45'00" ♉ – 06°41'15" ♉
6:	06°41'15" ♉ – 07°37'30" ♉

Nourishment comes in a multitude of forms to meet physical, mental, emotional and spiritual needs. Honoring the old adage of "Physician heal thyself" as a precursor to assisting anyone else! Balancing between care-giving and care-taking.

Selfishness

Self-sacrificing ⬦ Selfish : Altruism :: Selflessness

27.1 Nurturing Yourself: Taking care of Number One!
You take charge of your own well-being, or tend to give all your attention to other people's.

⊙: Your power to care means you easily take responsibility for all your own needs as a priority.

⊕: Always seeing others' care as more important than your own is an easy way to be depleted.

27.2 Being Accountable: Taking good care of yourself and your needs is natural.
You either nourish your needs, or generate a reliance on others to provide resources for you.

☾: A great reservoir of caring and resources is available between all lives in many ways.

♂: You tend to make demands that other people fulfill many of your requirements in life.

27.3 Being Resourceful: Recognizing who and what is nourishing in any situation.
Your constant search for nourishment often looks for it needlessly, and in unsuitable places.

⚷: You undergo transformation through indulging personal needs on many levels.

♂: You may have a drive to indulge yourself in ways that rarely bring nourishment.

27.4 Being Bounteous: Supporting everyone through giving and receiving.
You sometimes need an objective view of others' lives to find how to disburse your resources.

♃: Your generous disposition to nourish others comes from your own inner well-being.

♂: Your drive to provide for everyone can easily deplete yours' and others' resources.

27.5 Disbursing: Handling resources for the greatest benefits.
You easily distribute nourishment for everyone's benefit, or get overwhelmed by demands.

♃: You have the power and principle to effortlessly care for the well-being of others.

♄: You need to retain your balance in the face of seemingly endless demands for caring.

27.6 Providing Guardianship: Qualifying the use of all nourishing resources.
Successful steps imply flourishing outcomes so long as you honor yourself and your journey.

☾: Your holistic approach provides caring through all aspects of any healing process.

⚷: Transformation that comes through applying stringent codes of caring.

28

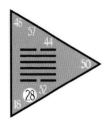

大過

The Game Player (of Life.)

Persistence
Honoring the courage and tenacity needed to meet life's personal challenges.

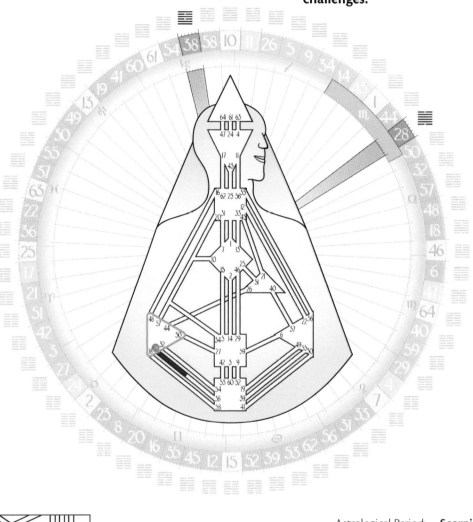

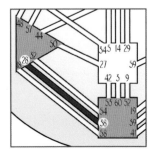

Part of Channel 28-38
The Channel of Struggle

Center: **Spleen**   Circuit: **Individual/Knowing**

Astrological Period: **Scorpio** ♏

Astrological Positions:

	02°00'00" ♏	– 07°37'30" ♏
1:	02°00'00" ♏	– 02°56'15" ♏
2:	02°56'15" ♏	– 03°52'30" ♏
3:	03°52'30" ♏	– 04°48'45" ♏
4:	04°48'45" ♏	– 05°45'00" ♏
5:	05°45'00" ♏	– 06°41'15" ♏
6:	06°41'15" ♏	– 07°37'30" ♏

By acknowledging the fear of dying, and finding your inner equilibrium, you hold true to your own standards among all the unbalancing forces of the world. You triumph when you combine Presence and Commitment in playing the game of life... and remember, life is a celebration!

Purposelessness
Purposeless ⬦ Gambling : Totality :: Immortality

28.1 Offering: Being intuitively open to deal with challenges.
Attuning to the needs of the moment you attend to either useful or to unhelpful factors.

♂: You have a drive to use anything that might assist in handling life's challenges.

♀: You engage your need for harmony rather than encountering the needs of a moment directly.

28.2 A Friend In Need: Finding & offering assistance in tough times in unusual places.
You fulfill all needs by aligning yourself with any source that is willing to cooperate with you.

☉: You intuit where to find the best assistance whether you make 'obvious' choices or not.

♃: Your expansive nature may forego personal principles when under pressure.

28.3 Being Rash: Relying on an unknowable future.
Acting brashly or fearfully can cause you to lose touch with your present reality.

♄: You have the self discipline to listen to your intuition for guidance, especially in times of struggle.

♃: Your promotional nature tends to favor external realities over personal intuitive guidance.

28.4 Being Strong: Finding extra inner resources to learn and grow.
Either you combine your intuitive gifts with your inner strength, or you collapse under duress.

♃: Your intuitive depth embraces difficulties and touches others' lives by personal example.

☿: Confusion is almost guaranteed by attempting to think your way through difficulties.

28.5 Trusting: Relating clearly with your present environment.
You can intuitively honor your reality, or attempt to restructure it and cause it to collapse.

☋: By intuiting how to bypass problems you bring transformation to everyone involved.

☉: By constantly seeking personal benefits in your life, you appear to be unreliable to others.

28.6 Grandeur: A tendency to "get in over your head."
Holding high ideals makes you reluctant to put up with personally degrading circumstances.

☋: The deeply, essential transformative drive to "win" in the game of life, regardless.

♆: Irrational fears can trigger depression, reminding you to relate again to your constant truth.

29

習坎 Commitment
The automatic "Yes!"
Sincere, patient perseverance provides the basis for success.

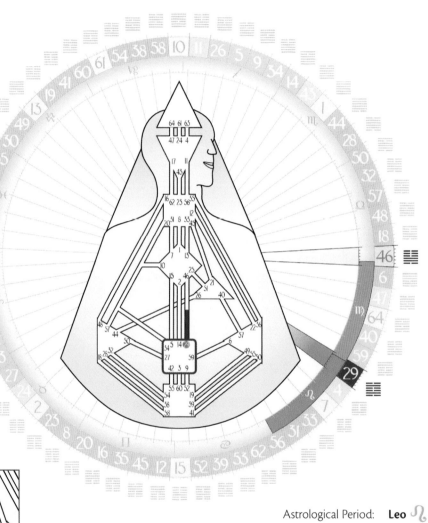

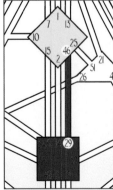

Part of Channel 29-46

The Channel of Discovery

Center: **Sacral**   Circuit: **Collective/Sensing**

Astrological Period: **Leo** ♌
                       Virgo ♍

Astrological Positions:

24°30'00" ♌ – 00°07'30" ♍

1:	24°30'00" ♌ – 25°26'15" ♌
2:	25°26'15" ♌ – 26°22'30" ♌
3:	26°22'30" ♌ – 27°18'45" ♌
4:	27°18'45" ♌ – 28°15'00" ♌
5:	28°15'00" ♌ – 29°11'15" ♌
6:	29°11'15" ♌ – 00°07'30" ♍

No matter how dark or dangerous aspects of our life appear to be,
there is always a way through. Never give up and never be manipulated!
Establishing for yourself the art of making right commitments for
each situation that confronts you. Trust your Authority!

Half-Heartedness
Unreliable ⟨⟩ Over-committing : Commitment :: Devotion

29.1 Being Cautious: Wondering if you can succeed will cause you to wobble.
Responding to situations, according to only what is *genuinely* needed, or else inviting trouble.

♂: Driving yourself to act only according to the requirements of any specific situation.

♆: Your hesitation to commit yourself only because of past problems will cause more trouble.

29.2 Advancing Slowly: A contentment with gradual achievements.
Your endeavors are sustained by proceeding directly and gradually, or undone by rushing.

☉: The nature of saying "Yes!" with the power to persist regardless of circumstances.

♀: Blinding yourself to real commitments allows you to maintain a sense of harmony.

29.3 Holding Out: Allowing decisiveness for change to come in its own natural way.
Finding that caution gives perspective over life's urgencies, you still feel an impulse to proceed.

♂: Realizing how important your clarity is to be able to commit decisively in your life.

♃: An inability to make commitments due to your expanded, even unrealistic sense of caution.

29.4 Committing: Being clear about your challenges brings relief quickly.
Embracing opportunities to move into any openings life offers, you experience rapid changes.

♄: You have the discipline to commit yourself totally to the simplest and most direct processes.

♀: To avoid difficulties by down-playing their relevance, you can miss opportunities in your life.

29.5 Being Restrained: Moving into and through a cycle with clarity.
Your clear commitment is enough to avoid excesses; otherwise you get exhausted by indulging.

☉: The clear responsiveness to say "Yes!" with a persistence that somehow brings completion.

⊕: A tendency to say "yes" blindly and without the inner clarity to evaluate what is involved.

29.6 Entangling: Clearing your path in front and behind.
You have an ability to get involved in anything, anytime, or you can choose to wait for clarity!

♂: The power to persevere that makes no sense often allows you to realize your goals.

♃: You over-commit despite the inevitable problems that arise from promises unkept.

30

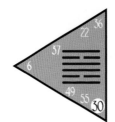

離 **Desires**
The Clinging Fire
By fully experiencing feelings you
come to sense the elusive qualities
of desires.

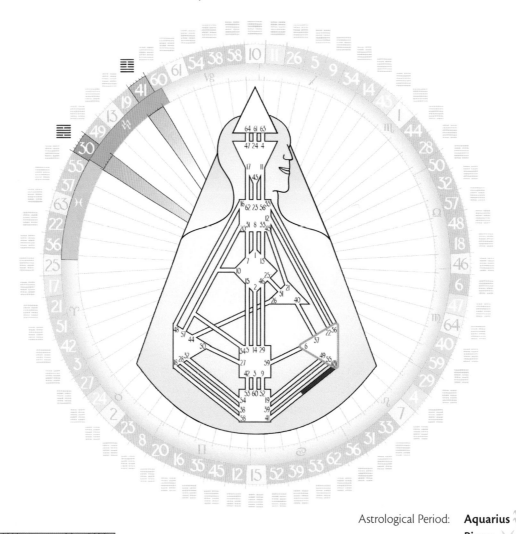

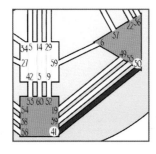

Part of Channel 30-41
The Channel of Recognition

Center: **Emotional**   Circuit: **Collective/
Sensing**

Astrological Period: **Aquarius** ♒
Pisces ♓

Astrological Positions:
24°30'00" ♒ – 00°07'30" ♓

1:	24°30'00" ♒ – 25°26'15" ♒
2:	25°26'15" ♒ – 26°22'30" ♒
3:	26°22'30" ♒ – 27°18'45" ♒
4:	27°18'45" ♒ – 28°15'00" ♒
5:	28°15'00" ♒ – 29°11'15" ♒
6:	29°11'15" ♒ – 00°07'30" ♓

There are two ways of experiencing the fires of desire : Cleansing or Immolation. Cleansing comes through witnessing total engagement with all life experiences. Immolation happens when you engage half-heartedly and become consumed by the sensations of experiences half-lived.
The call for totality!

Desire
Flippant ◇ Over-serious : Lightness :: Rapture

30.1 Clarifying: Finding inner balance whenever feelings stir.

As your feelings arise there is a moment to relate to them clearly or be overwhelmed by them.

☉: Inner sureness and stability allows you to ride all feelings, no matter what the situation.

♃: You recognize your changing feelings but have trouble disidentifying with them.

30.2 Finding The Golden Mean: Moderating between extremes of feelings.

Clarity comes by finding the "golden thread" between the highs and lows of an emotional wave.

☉: The strength to be true to your feelings and find considerate, natural ways to express them.

♂: Expressing feelings and desires regardless of the effects they have on yourself and others.

30.3 Keeping Your Cool: Going beyond desires by going through them.

"All things must pass," and you honor the acceptance or regret when acknowledging this.

☋: A persistently moderate yet steady approach to confronting trials brings you great rewards.

♃: Recognizing that life predictably brings you great waves of both exhilaration and despair.

30.4 Pacing: Enduring potential meltdowns and moving on.

Finalizing certain passages of life conclusively, alerts you to refresh, rebuild and realign.

☋: The deep intensity of feelings that impels you through experiences as transformations.

♃: You may express runaway feelings that bring exhaustion without satisfaction.

30.5 Heartsease: Acknowledging that embracing adversity enriches your life.

Balancing between feelings that bring you growth and surrendering to the will of Existence.

♃: The openness to explore your true feelings in depth before judging or acting on them.

☋: Transformation comes through releasing feelings that never bring you fulfillment.

30.6 Being Purified: Self acceptance and the clarity to release emotional expectations.

You either embrace feelings and release, or succumb to their inherent problems.

♂: Driven to eliminate negative feelings you encourage others to do the same.

☾: Moodiness makes it difficult to distinguish between your healthy and unhealthy feelings.

31

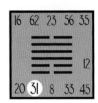

咸 **Influence**

I lead...because...
Mutual attractions and your readiness
to interrelate allow you to express your
natural influence.

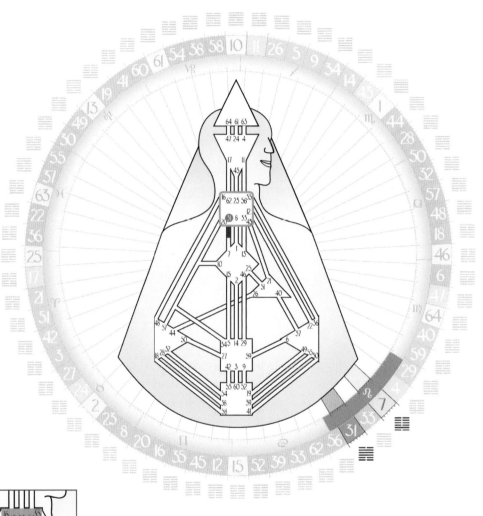

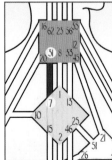

Part of Channel 7-31
The Channel of the Alpha
Center: **Throat**   Circuit: **Collective/Logic**

Astrological Period: **Leo** ♌
Astrological Positions:

02°00'00" ♌ – 07°37'30" ♌

1:	02°00'00" ♌ – 02°56'15" ♌
2:	02°56'15" ♌ – 03°52'30" ♌
3:	03°52'30" ♌ – 04°48'45" ♌
4:	04°48'45" ♌ – 05°45'00" ♌
5:	05°45'00" ♌ – 06°41'15" ♌
6:	06°41'15" ♌ – 07°37'30" ♌

> The potential to provide guidance and instruction align you and others with future prospects. It is important to relate from your own independent vision of reality.
>
> Arrogance
> Deferring ⬦ Arrogant : Leadership :: Humility

31

31.1 Opening: Finding the sincerity to allow yourself to be influential.
You either offer your ideals in simple ways or through contrived means.

⊙: You express leadership through clear alignment with your inherent aims.

⊕: Attempting to establish influential roles you might align with status rather than ideals.

31.2 Acting Independently: Attuning to the correct time to act.
Your independence is influential when you move to your own perception of timing.

♃: Your influence grows because of your trust in your own inner guidance.

☿: Confusion stems from a mental push to be influential that cannot wait for real clarity.

31.3 Distinguishing: Observing any impulse to influence others.
You need to be clear in yourself to find mutual influence and benefit in all dealings with others.

⊙: Your capacity to lead is enhanced by inner clarity and associations with worthy influences.

♃: A yearning to lead often exposes you to the influences of unhelpful company.

31.4 Convincing: All influence is realized according to its openness and purity of intent.
A sincere and clear heart allows you to influence others from your inner certainty.

☾: You are highly regarded for your heartfelt capacity to take charge in all situations.

♂: You can persuade others in ways that are not necessarily aligned with their actual needs.

31.5 Being Farsighted: Holding the intention to assert influence for bright outcomes.
Clear outcomes can be affirmed through your inner certainty or as a matter of fixed discipline.

⊙: Power comes through recognizing your own stance in influencing and being influenced.

☾: Any moodiness limits your influence, making it difficult at times to connect with the world.

31.6 Being Diligent: Relating your influence in the world from your own depth.
Intellectual comments rarely have much effect, whether you seek to influence others or not.

⊙: Being clear in your own life and influencing others by living according to your vision.

☾: A tendency to guide others dogmatically rather than trusting your own innate intelligence.

32 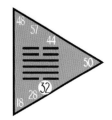 恆 Duration

Continuity and Change: Endurance
The only reliable feature of life is change,
giving everyone the need to constantly
adapt to the latest circumstances.

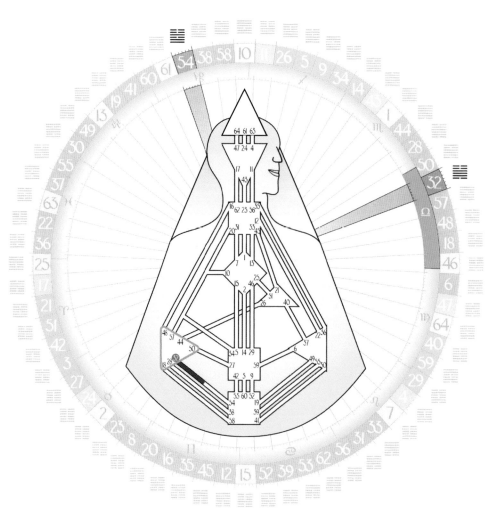

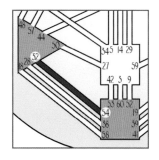

Part of Channel 32-54

The Channel of Transformation

Center: **Spleen** Circuit: **Tribal/Entrepreneurial**

Astrological Period: **Libra** ♎

Astrological Positions:

20°45'00" ♎ – 26°22'30" ♎

1:	20°45'00" ♎	– 21°41'15" ♎
2:	21°41'15" ♎	– 22°37'30" ♎
3:	22°37'30" ♎	– 23°33'45" ♎
4:	23°33'45" ♎	– 24°30'00" ♎
5:	24°30'00" ♎	– 25°26'15" ♎
6:	25°26'15" ♎	– 26°22'30" ♎

All adjustments that you make to your life's endeavors are tested by time, leading to the realization that endurance is a vital asset.

Failure

Disjointed ⬦ Fundamentalist : Conservation :: Veneration

32

32.1 Being Consistent: Lasting results require a constancy in your attitude.
Adapting your life style to change is a process requiring intent and attention to each moment.

☉: The bright nature to apply your attention to all aspects of a transforming process.

♂: Achieving results you override the instincts that assist you to resolve difficulties.

32.2 Avoiding extremes: Holding a steady course.
You are either alert during times of change, or become confused by interacting with others.

♀: Your natural approach to dealing with changes brings benefits for everyone concerned.

♃: Your sensitivity to complaints causes you to pursue unnecessary and untimely changes.

32.3 Withstanding: Using your inner guidance when distracted by change.
Your steady or casual approach to taking on changes determines your ability to adapt to them.

☿: All times of transformation require you remain clear to your inner, enduring intentions.

♃: Making problems out to be bigger than they are limits your alertness in times of change.

32.4 Being Realistic: Re-evaluating your needs clearly.
Being true to your overall goals gives you added confidence when challenged by changes.

♃: Your inner optimism endorses your own principles and adaptability in times of change.

♄: An inner practicality adapts your principles to the needs of any challenging situations.

32.5 Complying: Staying aligned with changes.
You need to interact creatively in all of life's changing and challenging situations.

☾: Your shifting sense of the nature of change brings easy adaptation to all phases of life.

♂: Your impatience with life's timing makes you inventive in finding ways to force the pace.

32.6 Witnessing: Impassively observing your world even as you move in it.
You have a need to accept change or else live in fear of being continually overwhelmed by life.

♅: Your deep alignment with the forces of change allows you to merge into transformation.

♆: Overwhelmed by anxiety you'll fail to find meaning in change. A great need to stay present.

33

Retreat

Withdrawal: Privacy & Secrets:
"I remember"

You assimilate life experiences and recharge your whole Being by withdrawing, whether on physical, mental, emotional or spiritual levels.

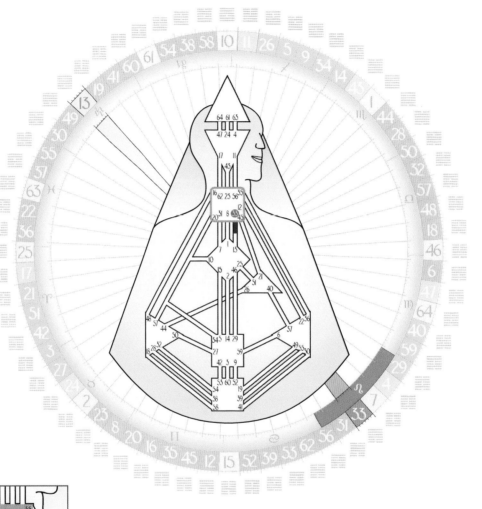

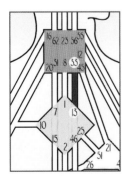

Part of Channel 13-33

The Channel of the Prodigal

Center: **Throat**   Circuit: **Collective/Sensing**

Astrological Period: **Leo** ♌

Astrological Positions:

07°37'30" ♌ – 13°15'00" ♌

1:	07°37'30" ♌ – 08°33'45" ♌
2:	08°33'45" ♌ – 09°30'00" ♌
3:	09°30'00" ♌ – 10°26'15" ♌
4:	10°26'15" ♌ – 11°22'30" ♌
5:	11°22'30" ♌ – 12°18'45" ♌
6:	12°18'45" ♌ – 13°15'00" ♌

More happens in the course of a day than you can process in a night's sleep. You are the natural storyteller who holds the threads of narratives in many realms of experience.

Forgetting

Reserved ◇ Censorious : Mindfulness :: Revelation

33.1 Observing: Remaining calm when there is no advantage in becoming involved.
If you remember your inner serenity you have the clarity to commit to an experience or not.

☉: You have the sense to retreat rather than commit to experiences that are destabilizing.

♂: You tend to rush into situations that have little merit, only to be overwhelmed by them.

33.2 Unshakeable: Steadfast in your belief that everything works out as it should.
Rather than be overwhelmed, you can retreat and wait for your own time of strength to come.

♃: Saving your energy during times of recession, in readiness for any change in fortunes.

♆: By submitting to any beliefs in personal failure, you can lose trust in yourself.

33.3 Dis-connecting: The uplifting sense of quick recovery when you retreat.
Putting aside any fears and anxieties, you realize the advantages in retreating.

♃: Your expansive nature recognizes the great benefits in having times to yourself.

♂: Your personal compulsion to be private at any cost will easily estrange others.

33.4 Detaching: Avoiding unnecessary constraints. (A potential to access past lives).
Watching life on many levels, your inner stillness craves external calm.

☾: You honor your sometimes dramatic need to retreat for regeneration and resurgence.

♆: If you lose touch with the present you can be swept up in all kinds of confusing scenarios.

33.5 Being Self-protective: The independence and clarity to disengage.
You either are clear in your need for privacy, or lose your poise through being overly helpful.

☾: You sense the importance of privacy and secrecy until the time is right to engage others.

♃: Randomly sharing yourself and your secrets brings you problems in the resulting confusion.

33.6 Letting go!: Moving on from moment to moment, from one scene to the next.
Being objective you take care to be refreshed and ready for all new experiences.

☉: Your bright nature is free from doubts and concerns about letting go of needless burdens.

♃: Your overgenerous nature is unable to completely let go and risks becoming codependent.

34

大壯 Power
Great Strength
Power is only great when its display or use comes from an inner balance.

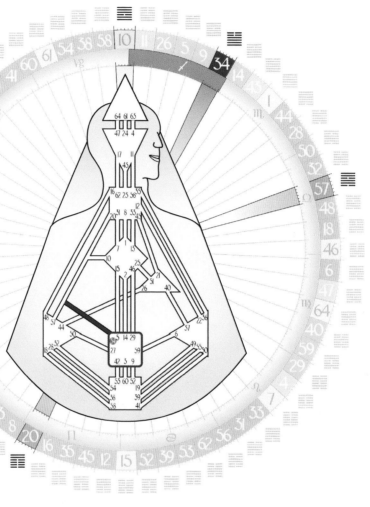

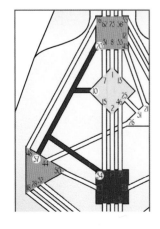

Part of Channel 10-34
The Channel of Exploration

Part of Channel 20-34
The Channel of Keeping Busy

Part of Channel 34-57
The Channel of Power

Center: **Sacral**   Circuit: **Individual/Integration/Knowing**

Astrological Period: **Sagitarius** ♐

Astrological Positions:

00°07'30" ♐ – 05°45'00" ♐

1:	00°07'30" ♐ – 01°03'45" ♐
2:	01°03'45" ♐ – 02°00'00" ♐
3:	02°00'00" ♐ – 02°56'15" ♐
4:	02°56'15" ♐ – 03°52'30" ♐
5:	03°52'30" ♐ – 04°48'45" ♐
6:	04°48'45" ♐ – 05°45'00" ♐

You persistently move your energy towards achieving what is empowering, appropriate and essential, and at the same time seek to avoid what might be considered to be aggressive and egoistic. The only asexual Sacral Gate.

Force

Self-effacing ◇ Pushy (Bullish) : Strength :: Majesty

34.1 Being Presumptive: Haphazard, sometimes clumsy use of power.
Using power well comes from your inner strength or calming reactions its use causes in others.
♄: You have the discipline to control how you use your power by examining your motives.
☋: Personal transformation usually comes through reactions to your use of power.

34.2 Being Temperate: Resistance lessens when you apply power carefully.
In times of success you either increase or lose your respect for others.
♂: You have the energy to continue in your efforts especially when success is sure.
♀: Always seeking admiration for your achievements saps your inner strength.

34.3 Estimating: Using power in accordance with prevailing conditions.
Using your power discreetly, or being overly zealous and attracting complications.
♄: You have the self-discipline to use your power in proportion to the situations at hand.
☿: By fabricating roles for how to use your power you find yourself reacting to reality.

34.4 Inner Strength: Maintaining inner balance assures achievement.
Trusting or doubting your inner clarity results in the success or failure of any effort.
☋: You power through any situation by aligning with your inner clarity and confidence.
♂: The potential for the abuse of power comes by ignoring your personal integrity.

34.5 Accepting: Nothing to prove in your easy use of power.
Seeing how your power affects others, you either embrace this or are uncomfortable with it.
♂: You have the strength and persistence to use power appropriately and when necessary.
☾: Being moody affects your consistent use of power and results in you being hesitant.

34.6 Being Careful: Having the wisdom to reassess.
Your discriminate or indiscriminate use of power means outcomes are harmonious or not.
⊕: You learn ways to adapt your use of power to maintain stability in any situation.
♃: Any extravagant use of your power may cause exhaustion for everyone around you.

35

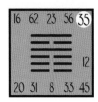

晉 **Progress**

Advancing: "And now for something completely different."

Seeking to qualify life by comparing all manner of experiences, there is an unceasing drive to explore every aspect of human nature.

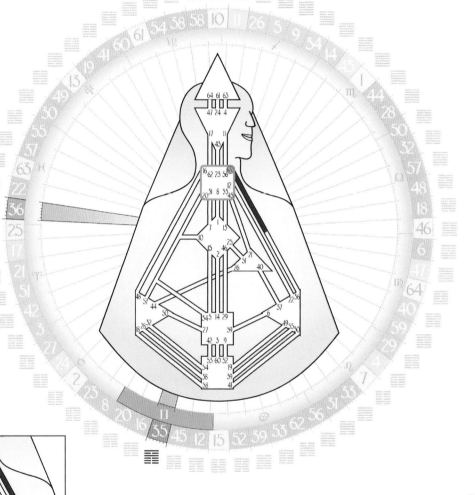

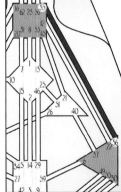

Part of Channel 35-36
The Channel of Versatility

Center: **Throat**   Circuit: **Collective/Sensing**

Astrological Period: **Gemini**

Astrological Positions:

11°22'30" – 17°00'00"

1:	11°22'30" – 12°18'45"
2:	12°18'45" – 13°15'00"
3:	13°15'00" – 14°01'15"
4:	14°01'15" – 15°07'30"
5:	15°07'30" – 16°03'45"
6:	16°03'45" – 17°00'00"

> You only need an experience once, and most often having the experience is actually the goal itself.

> Hunger
> Bored ◇ Manic : Adventure :: Boundlessness

35

35.1 Holding Steady: Accepting setbacks as part of life's process.
Whether you see yourself as right or not it is always possible to take rejection personally.

♀: Your inner harmony sees negation as a sign to refine your perception of experiences.

Ψ: It is easy for you to take any form of rejection as a personal failure and humiliation.

35.2 Growing: Every interaction brings potentially new experiences.
Sometimes your endeavors are held back until you are available to receive assistance.

♀: Inner balance and virtue help you cope with unproductive times until your inspiration returns.

☾: In a state of moodiness you can insist on progress whether the timing is right or not.

35.3 Combining: Sharing experiences with others.
Evolution comes when you fully experience life in the company and trust of others.

♃: Your expansive nature brings progressive change to your own and others' lives

☉: You tend to take a pivotal role in everything often disregarding other people's roles.

35.4 Being Impulsive: The yearning to demand progress at any cost.
Check you Authority when you are pushing for experiences without any obvious goals in sight.

☾: Your inner integrity recognizes the significance of change and the opportunities it brings.

♂: You push for excitement at any opportunity, sometimes precipitating crises.

35.5 Being Honorable: Tempering expectations in favor of progress.
You enhance experiences by giving of yourself, whether you feel personally benefited or not.

☿: You try to benefit everyone you involve in your life through your experience.

♃: Your generosity brings expansion for everyone, often without a sense of personal fulfillment.

35.6 Self-examining: A readiness to reexamine and realign your outward feelings.
Regretting any experience impels you to modify your ways, simply or with a complete overhaul.

♄: You have the self discipline to be fair with others when you implement change in their lives.

♂: Your drive to instruct other people in ways that change their lives can be unpopular.

36

明夷 **Crisis Resolution**
The Darkening of the Light
There's always a potential to feel a sense of crisis before you make a move to experience something for the first time.

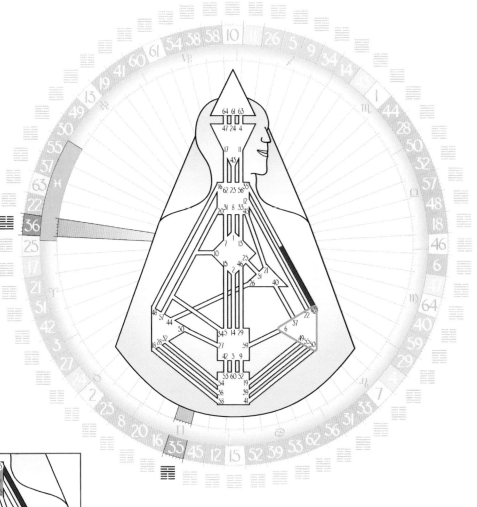

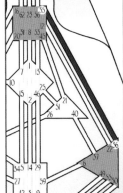

Part of Channel 35-36
The Channel of Versatility

Center: **Emotions** Circuit: **Collective/Sensing**

Astrological Period: **Pisces** ♓

Astrological Positions:

22°37′30″ ♓ − 28°15′00″ ♓

1:	22°37′30″ ♓ − 23°33′45″ ♓
2:	23°33′45″ ♓ − 24°30′00″ ♓
3:	24°30′00″ ♓ − 25°26′15″ ♓
4:	25°26′15″ ♓ − 26°22′30″ ♓
5:	26°22′30″ ♓ − 27°18′45″ ♓
6:	27°18′45″ ♓ − 28°15′00″ ♓

In its lowest form, crisis is debilitating and discouraging. In its highest form, inner brightness and outer gentility come together to live through every aspect of human experiencing. Once an experience is indulged, feelings flow through a full range of emotional highs and lows. Experiencing is subjective and ultimately impersonal.

Turbulence
Collapsed ◇ Crisis Prone : Humanity :: Compassion

36

36.1 Enduring: Reflecting inwards when challenged by outer circumstances.
Accepting or ignoring your feelings and holding true to yourself or not in critical times.

♂: You manage to handle emotional turmoil even while restraining your impulsive tendencies.

♃: If you magnify and externalize small difficulties you end up in constant turmoil.

36.2 Being Constant: Being loyal when challenged in the company of others.
Personal setbacks can give you the stimulation to help and receive help from others.

♆: You apply your imagination to further yourself and others through crisis situations.

☾: Any moodiness makes you vacillate in seeking or providing assistance during crises.

36.3 Breaking Out: Finding the point of transition from darkness to light.
You shift from crisis to resolution when you witness emotional habits that don't serve you.

☊: A transformative process in which you ride emotional crises to find your personal clarity

♃: You feel the great benefits of change but are reluctant to be done with old emotions.

36.4 Surveying: Accessing your way by following your own light through all situations.
Your way through life depends on you accessing your own inner clarity, or not, in all crises.

☊: You appreciate that secret and esoteric knowledge can help in resolving volatile situations.

☾: Your inner ability to see beyond obvious concerns and issues can assist anyone in crisis.

36.5 Shielding: Hiding your intentions from insensitive eyes.
Enduring disagreeable situations intelligently leads you to eventual fortune.

☊: Transformation is possible for you when you find the way to thrive in intense experiences.

☿: Confusing yourself and others you seek to resolve emotional scenarios with mental solutions.

36.6 Being Resolved: Committing to persist in what is right.
Darkness is an absence of light. When truth is revealed all aspects of untruth begin to dissipate.

♃: Your powerful alignment with pure emotion brings natural healing and transformation.

♄: Your reluctance to resolve crises makes you persist in finding some problem or another.

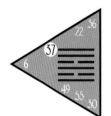

37

家人 **Family**
Friendship (Community)
Whether on a spiritual, community or family level, clear interrelationships are necessary for the stability and well-being of everyone.

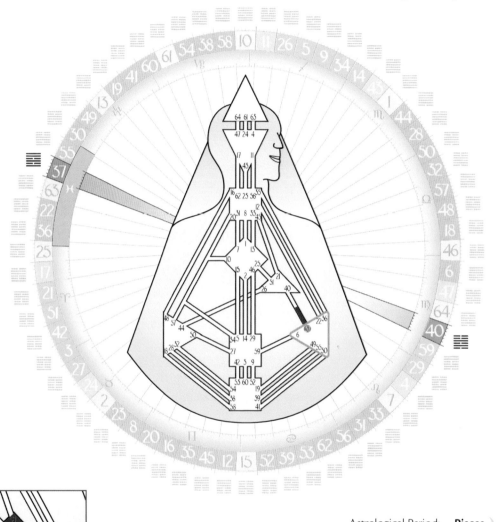

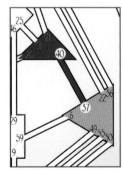

Part of Channel 37-40
The Channel of Community

Center: **Emotions**   Circuit: **Tribal/ Community**

Astrological Period: **Pisces** ♓

Astrological Positions:

	05°45'00" ♓ – 11°22'30" ♓
1:	05°45'00" ♓ – 06°41'15" ♓
2:	06°41'15" ♓ – 07°37'30" ♓
3:	07°37'30" ♓ – 08°33'45" ♓
4:	08°33'45" ♓ – 09°30'00" ♓
5:	09°30'00" ♓ – 10°26'15" ♓
6:	10°26'15" ♓ – 11°22'30" ♓

37

> Familiarity within a family, whether its members are recognized through blood-relationship, community or business, is exercised through touch and food. Family is the foundation of community ethics and all community accomplishments.
>
> Weakness
> Over-sentimental ◇ Cruel : Equality :: Tenderness

37.1 Revering: Respect and honor is due to the innately wise.
Being considerate in your own attitudes encourages others to be attentive in theirs.
♀: Through harmony and friendliness you provide a solid basis for all relationships.
♂: If you take a competitive stance you can lose your inherent friendliness and compatibility.

37.2 Being Self-sufficient: Achievements are enhanced through synergy.
You endorse personal responsibility as the foundation for a community's strength.
♃: By taking full responsibility for your own life, you profoundly alter the would around you.
☿: You might attempt to save the world by emphasizing the shortcomings of others.

37.3 Moderating: A steady reserve supports communal well-being.
In disagreements there is a need for authority and fairness to bring the family back together.
♃: Your expansive and generous sensitivity supports open and clear relationships.
♂: Emotional imbalance makes you more concerned to keep order than acknowledge feelings.

37.4 Enriching: Supporting the family's prosperity.
You emphasize that the well-being of families involves everyone's presence and contributions.
☾: You further the well-being of your world through all your clear contributions.
♄: Your particular view of family is prone to approve only traditional ways and views.

37.5 Being Loyal: Natural and magnanimous devotion to the family.
You forgive all transgressions within the family unless you feel that you are being used.
♀: Your selfless affection enhances the love and harmony felt among everyone around you.
♂: You can lean on others for emotional support while still disliking any signs of dependency.

37.6 Being Astute: Holding high personal standards encourages others to do the same.
Being true to your own feelings of responsibility ensures your ability to benefit everyone.
♀: You recognize and enhance all the qualities of life possible through harmonious friendships.
☿: Your restless nature often craves diverse friendships beyond the boundaries of the family.

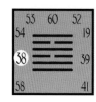

Opposition
The Fighter
An individual stands against
perceived untruth.

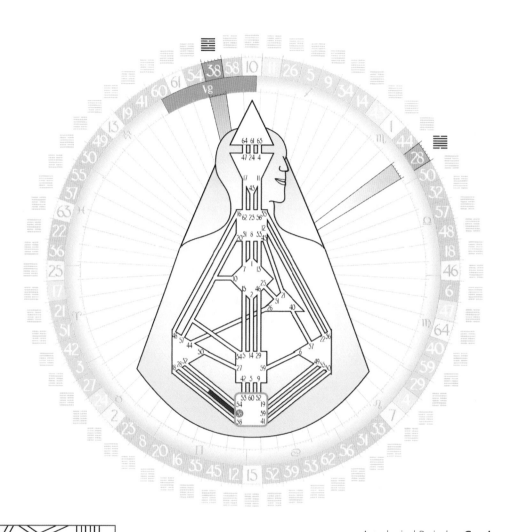

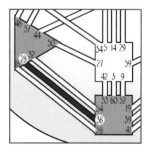

Part of Channel 28-38
The Channel of Struggle

Center: **Root**   Circuit: **Individual/Knowing**

Astrological Period: **Capricorn** Vg

Astrological Positions:

09°30'00" Vg – 15°07'30" Vg

1:	09°30'00" Vg – 10°26'15" Vg
2:	10°26'15" Vg – 11°22'30" Vg
3:	11°22'30" Vg – 12°18'45" Vg
4:	12°18'45" Vg – 13°15'00" Vg
5:	13°15'00" Vg – 14°11'15" Vg
6:	14°11'15" Vg – 15°07'30" Vg

The potential viewpoint that you must fight with the whole world when all you want is an individual's right to personal freedom.
The need to remember that we are One.

Struggle
Stubborn ⬦ Struggling : Perseverance :: Honor

38.1 Being Impartial: No need to worry when a situation can resolve itself.
Do you need be concerned with every complication in life, or want to struggle anyway?
Ψ: Deep attunement to your inner guidance knows when and how to deal with discomforts.
♂: Your drive to continuously fight with life causes you eventually to expand your intuition.

38.2 Being Courteous: A spirit of conciliation furthers your purpose.
Being relaxed in your attitude to others allows for the possibility to intuit your own purpose.
(ʘ): Transformation happens in diverse situations through you forcing yourself to be amenable.
☾: Your moodiness will accommodate others only grudgingly when you are challenged.

38.3 Being Tenacious: Accepting challenges as a part of your growth.
Staying true to what you know and who you trust aligns you in your quest for life's meaning.
☉: Contending with many difficulties you follow your own way to personal empowerment.
⊕: Being caught in contention as a way of life drains you and your helpers of all resources.

38.4 Rejoining: Turning away from being isolated in the face of adversity.
Trusting in your own process you can receive assistance during seemingly impossible situations.
(ʘ): You can hold out for the bright flash of opportunity that transforms everything.
♂: Beset by outside pressures, it's as though you have to struggle against the whole world.

38.5 Actualizing: Penetrating through misunderstandings by connecting with company.
You intuit when to stop and see who will help, or you can persist in your apparent isolation.
♄: You have discipline to stop and review your contentious stance and recognize your allies.
(ʘ): Transformation happens when you are first isolated then supported in personal struggles.

38.6 Mis-trusting: Fighting with shadows.
Dealing with diversity takes time and your willingness. Fighting with life itself is also possible.
♄: Your disciplined nature embraces life after examining your constant tendency to struggle.
⊕: If you identify with struggle due to a distrust of the world, you amplify needless tensions.

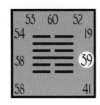

甈 Provocation

Hardship

Finding a way through obstacles of all sorts opens you to challenges that promote personal growth.

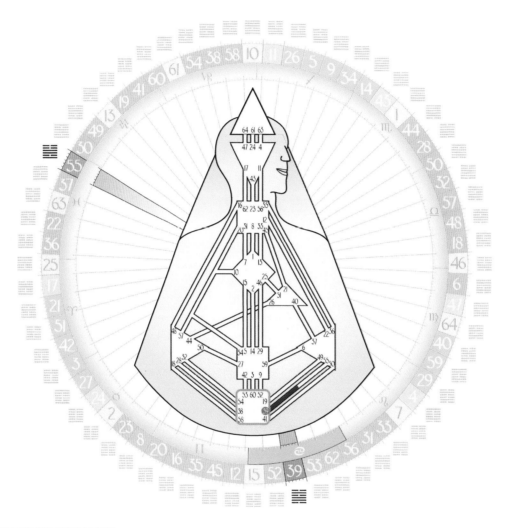

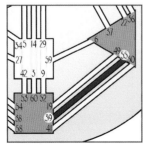

Part of Channel 39-55

The Channel of Emoting

Center: **Root** Circuit: **Individual/Knowing**

Astrological Period: **Cancer** ♋

Astrological Positions:

09°30'00" ♋ – 15°07'30" ♋

1:	09°30'00" ♋	– 10°26'15" ♋
2:	10°26'15" ♋	– 11°22'30" ♋
3:	11°22'30" ♋	– 12°18'45" ♋
4:	12°18'45" ♋	– 13°15'00" ♋
5:	13°15'00" ♋	– 14°11'15" ♋
6:	14°11'15" ♋	– 15°07'30" ♋

The outer and inner reflect each other perfectly. If you are perplexed by the way in which your world mirrors you, look within yourself to find the source of that reflection. Provoking or being provoked is not the same as fighting.

Provocation

Trapped ⬦ Provocative : Dynamism :: Liberation

39.1 Being Detached: Dropping any need for forced interactions.

Whether you engage with anyone directly or not, often you provoke people without trying.

♂: You have the means to avoid any imposed obstacles by acting in your own way and time.

☿: Your indecision about when and how to deal with obstacles can make others hopping mad.

39.2 Encountering: Engaging adversity as a means to self-discovery.

You learn to 'Grab the bull by the horns,' whether it feels comfortable to do so or not.

☾: You naturally provoke life, so you are constantly called on to meet situations face to face.

♃: Feeling intense discomfort with stressful upsets, you tend to seek alternative possibilities. (like: *"Beam me up, Scottie!"* or *"I'm outta here!"*)

39.3 Facing Challenge: Honoring your own way of dealing with trials.

Reconsidering or not, your internal push to engage with or avoid external confrontations.

♃: Your expansive stance does not absorb or give off a sense of fear when in confrontations.

⊕: Justifying how you confront all obstacles you limit the possibility for fresh alternatives.

39.4 Converging: Finding unifying elements before taking any action.

Awaiting right opportunities to handle confrontations is not always the easiest thing for you.

☾: By perceiving the essence of obstructions you find the energy to deal with them.

☉: You tend to tackle confrontations regardless of circumstances or outcomes.

39.5 Finding Assistance: By facing obstacles directly, help becomes available.

You either allow yourself to find assistance in difficult times or stay doggedly self-sufficient.

♆: You somehow draw any assistance you need to find ways to bypass all obstacles.

♂: Your insistence to take on confrontations as a permanent agenda is exasperating to others.

39.6 Troubleshooting: The natural gift for solving problems.

Some people enjoy having their problems, so fixing their problems can really upset them.

☾: You are sensitive to the overall needs of situations before attempting to solve any problems.

♂: If you always take on problems regardless of facts you can end up causing greater problems!

40

解 **Deliverance**
Freedom for yourself and from any hardship.
Using willpower to distinguish the difference between struggle and liberation you attain what you want.

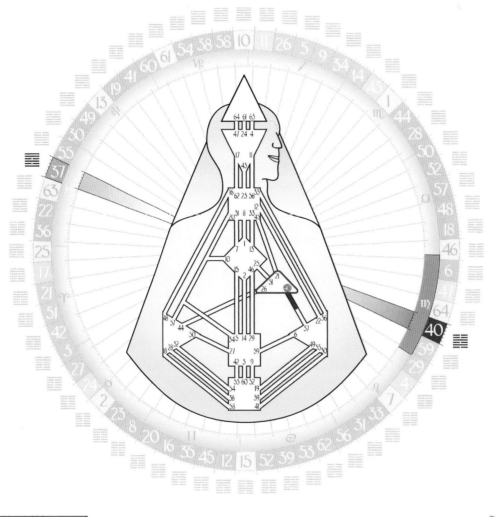

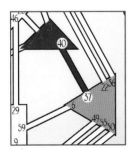

Part of Channel 37-40
The Channel of Community

Center: **Heart**   Circuit: **Tribal/Community**

Astrological Period: **Virgo** ♍
Astrological Positions:

05°45′00″ ♍ – 11°22′30″ ♍

1:	05°45′00″ ♍ – 06°41′15″ ♍
2:	06°41′15″ ♍ – 07°37′30″ ♍
3:	07°37′30″ ♍ – 08°33′45″ ♍
4:	08°33′45″ ♍ – 09°30′00″ ♍
5:	09°30′00″ ♍ – 10°26′15″ ♍
6:	10°26′15″ ♍ – 11°22′30″ ♍

Willful heart energy is exerted to accomplish great feats efficiently...
and then requires rest in detachment and separateness to recover
and digest what has transpired.
"Freedom from" becomes "Freedom for," becomes "Freedom!"
Exhaustion
Permissive ⬦ Contemptuous : Resolve :: Higher will

40.1 Recovering: The prime need for a hard-working heart is rest.

After any achievement is complete, you can best consolidate your situation by resting.

☉: Your find ways to enjoy your aloneness and find relaxation after exertions.

☾: Your changing moods can make you question your achievements and miss the call to rest.

40.2 Being Conclusive: Moving beyond potentially limiting life qualities.

Clearly finding your own way in tricky situations assures your ability to handle any disruptions.

☉: You have the natural willingness to be true to yourself, regardless of distractions.

☾: Your sensitivity makes it hard to avoid the situations that hamper your very freedom.

40.3 Being Whole: Matching your lifestyle with your unruffled inner being.

If you make a display of ego willpower you easily attract problematic company and situations.

♅: You have an ability to 'go it alone' and induce transformation through the use of willpower.

♂: Any drive involving your ego expression will get you the kind of attention you do not want!

40.4 Reality checks: Honestly viewing a tendency to include unrealistic partnerships.

Perceptions change constantly and you need to drop all alliances that limit your freedom.

☋: You bypass problems when you only encourage those who have similar aspirations to you.

♂: You may persist with old friendships and habits long after their relevance is exhausted.

40.5 Liberating: Being clear in your separation from outside interference.

In a world full of hazards you require that all of your associations are supportive and relevant.

☋: You have the confidence to let go of relationships that hamper your freedom.

⊕: You trade your liberation for the support of people who often interfere in your life.

40.6 Definitive Stance: Freedom is realized through conclusive removal of obstacles.

You overcome your own reluctance to be free and remove anyone and anything impeding you.

☉: Your clear conviction purposely removes all barriers that hamper your liberation.

⊕: Removing obstacles as a role in life can cause you to use unnecessarily severe measures.

41

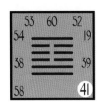

損 **Imagination**
Evaluating potentials
Living within limiting resources gives
occasion for dreams and fantasies to
arise.

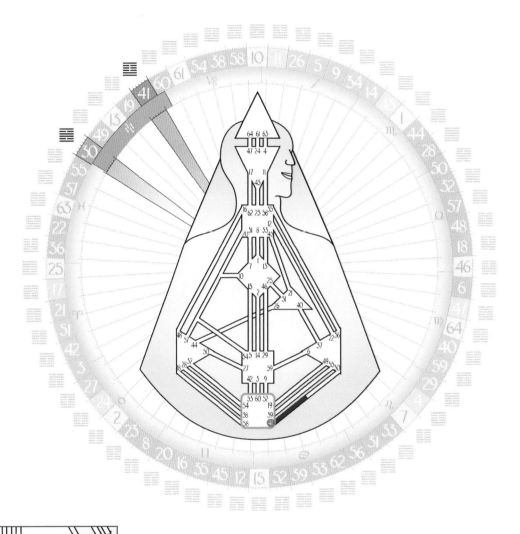

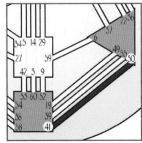

Part of Channel 30-41
The Channel of Recognition

Center: **Root**   Circuit: **Collective/Sensing**

Astrological Period: **Aquarius** ♒

Astrological Positions:

02°00'00" ♒ – 07°37'30" ♒

1:	02°00'00" ♒ – 02°56'15" ♒
2:	02°56'15" ♒ – 03°52'30" ♒
3:	03°52'30" ♒ – 04°48'45" ♒
4:	04°48'45" ♒ – 05°45'00" ♒
5:	05°45'00" ♒ – 06°41'15" ♒
6:	06°41'15" ♒ – 07°37'30" ♒

In the search to be fulfilled you look into any potential experiences that might move you through a cycle from emptiness to accomplishment. Dreaming opens doorways to experiences that bring satisfaction and completion, or endless fantasies that are self-sustaining. Existence was created when we fell in love with emptiness.

Fantasy

Dreamy (Spacey) ◇ Hyperactive : Anticipation :: Emanation

41.1 Moderating: Finding the balance between giving and receiving.
Being either centered and clear, or headstrong in your handling of how you use your energies.

♆: Your creative imagination streams resources in ways that benefit yourself and others.

☿: Confusion with your role and resources leads you into difficulties at the outset of endeavors.

41.2 Giving and Receiving: Being recognized for the services you render.
By indulging others without diminishing yourself, you find rewards in fulfilling endeavors.

♄: You have the discipline to watch out for yourself while considering others' needs.

♂: By demanding attention and reward for assisting others you eventually diminish yourself.

41.3 Synergizing: Experiences are fulfilling because of right alliances.
In all your life experiences there's a need to select suitable company and essential resources

♄: You choose partnerships that endure through times of separation and aloneness.

☾: Your changeable nature seeks mixed company to share in your resources and dreams.

41.4 Examining Shortcomings: Diminishing your poor habits increases your fortunes.
By acknowledging what does not fulfill, you begin to attract fresh resources and experiences.

⊕: Having humility to clear up your personal problems opens the way for assistance to come.

♀: You might unrealistically expect assistance from others to rectify your own shortcomings.

41.5 Being Recognized: Inner clarity ensures rewards.
Watching how you and others deal with constraints, whether you find completion or not.

♂: You push to clarify the essential attitudes that will promote your fullness of purpose.

♀: You tend to see a half full glass as half empty, despite sensing how fortunate you are.

41.6 Being Fulfilled: Bringing benefits to others while expanding your own resources.
You enrich everyone through your inner watchfulness and your selective ways.

♄: Your disciplined view enhances your own resources and also bring expansion for others

⟨ʘ⟩: You tend to avoid public attention but have the power to shift constraints into great gains.

42

Increase
Benefiting
Steadily growing your inner and outer resources expands all experiences for yourself and others.

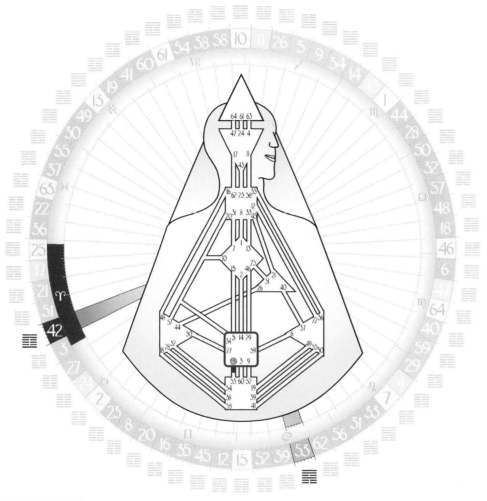

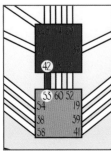

Part of Channel 42-53
Channel of Cycles

Center: **Sacral**   Circuit: **Collective/Sensing**

Astrological Period: **Aries** ♈

Astrological Positions:

20°45'00" ♈ – 26°22'30" ♈

1:	20°45'00" ♈ – 21°41'15" ♈
2:	21°41'15" ♈ – 22°37'30" ♈
3:	22°37'30" ♈ – 23°33'45" ♈
4:	23°33'45" ♈ – 24°30'00" ♈
5:	24°30'00" ♈ – 25°26'15" ♈
6:	25°26'15" ♈ – 26°22'30" ♈

Finding your own wholesome, balanced and naturally timed growth in your life encourages you to respond to all manner of experiences that come to you. Dispassionately watching how you catalyze growth, you may ultimately benefit from your efforts in others' lives.

Expectation

Grasping ⬦ Flaky : Detachment :: Celebration

42.1 Accomplishing: Great deeds are possible.

You question your confidence to expand in many directions on behalf of yourself and others.

☉: You align with an inner confidence and certainty that grows in all areas of life.

♀: Becoming distracted by the needs of others you can end up "spreading yourself too thin."

42.2 Blessing: Inner attunement with what is beneficial.

Being steadfast in sustaining your clear intentions you receive tangential benefits.

☉: By recognizing your way and staying true to it you find much reward and acclaim.

♀: Unless watchful, you are easily overwhelmed by the effects of others' demands.

42.3 Being Competent: Great wisdom is gained by learning from your ordeals.

There is nothing that cannot grow, if you patiently persevere with clarity.

♂: An unshakable certainty comes when you move gracefully through all trials and adversity.

☾: You may embrace moodiness that easily throws you into despair when problems arise.

42.4 Being Trustworthy: Giving sensible counsel that serves one and all.

Your opportunist nature often finds you mediating the fulfillment of growth for everyone.

☾: When you consider all aspects of growth you find the way for greatest accomplishments.

♀: Immaturity may place greater importance in company than in the company's achievements.

42.5 Being Kindhearted: Unselfish and clear aspirations bring fulfillment.

Acknowledgment is gained through your achievements in both personal and shared endeavors.

☉: Your inner strength and confident kindness benefits everyone in sustaining their growth.

♀: You place sincerity and sympathy with others as more important than your own growth.

42.6 Balancing: Maintaining a good mixture of giving and taking.

Successful steps imply flourishing outcomes so long as you honor yourself and your journey.

☾: You are sensible to sharing your own growth with others, ensuring the benefit of everyone.

♄: Remaining stuck in your own growth you may actually proceed to deplete everyone else.

夬 Breakthrough!
Insight
You receive new perceptions, and by remaining resolute, reform old ways and habits.

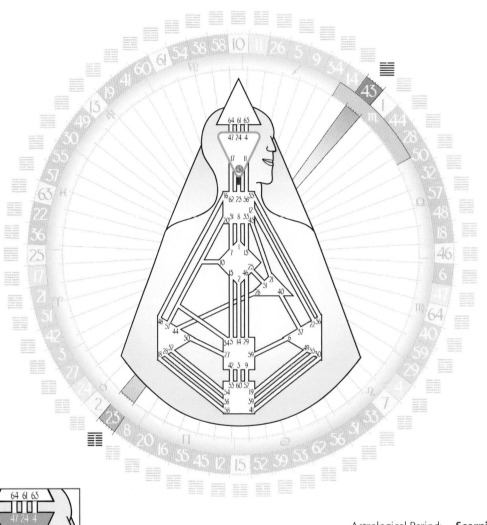

Part of Channel 23-43

The Channel of Structuring

Center: **Mind**   Circuit: **Individual/Knowing**

Astrological Period: **Scorpio** ♏

Astrological Positions:

	18°52'30" ♏	– 24°30'00" ♏
1:	18°52'30" ♏	– 19°48'15" ♏
2:	19°48'45" ♏	– 20°45'30" ♏
3:	20°45'00" ♏	– 21°41'45" ♏
4:	21°41'15" ♏	– 22°37'00" ♏
5:	22°37'30" ♏	– 23°33'15" ♏
6:	23°33'45" ♏	– 24°30'00" ♏

Great serenity is required to assimilate new concepts so that they can be delivered clearly. Paying attention to the bright spark that eliminates hesitation and promotes resolution. The Inner ear.

Deafness

Deaf ◇ Noisy : Insight :: Epiphany

43.1 Being Vigilant: No need to rush blindly into employing new insights.
Your resignation and intent are needed to replace old ways and implement any new insight.

ʘ: You need strong resolve to implement transformation from your insights.

♀: You have aesthetic admiration but sometimes a difficulty in implementing your insights.

43.2 Being Resolute: A clear mind gives access to clear outcomes.
Staying true or not to your way of relating insights affects whether they ever become a reality.

ʘ: You have an inbuilt means to assimilate insights that facilitates personal transformation.

☾: You tend to be actively engaged in avoiding anyone who might complicate your life.

43.3 Being Resilient: Standing your ground in implementing your way.
Your own resolve or insecurity relating to your personal insights, affects all facets of your life.

ʘ: When aligned with your insights you resist any criticism in achieving your purpose.

☾: You can become unsure of the soundness of your insights when challenged by others.

43.4 Being Restless: If you are unable to hear sage advice you remain indecisive.
It is hard to surrender to life circumstances when your mind emphatically craves change.

☿: You recognize the need to be objective when you consider implementing your insights.

♂: If you insist on implementing insights that are obviously not feasible, you will be distressed.

43.5 Being Forthright: Implementing any new insights requires great thoroughness.
You grow through implementing your personal insights, or succumb to irrelevant input.

☾: You have a sensibility to know the conditions in which your personal insights will work out.

♀: You have a hopeful expectation that others will readily agree with your fresh insights.

43.6 Redirecting: Fostering acceptable and practical growth from insights.
Your careful objectivity ensures that your insights will lead towards lasting transformation.

☉: You utilize your objectivity to review your insights and assure they are useful to others.

♂: If you are attached only to the brilliance of your insights you may easily become ostracized.

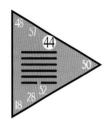

姤 Patterns

Meeting Together

In any meeting of likes or opposites, acceptance and mutual tolerance is essential.

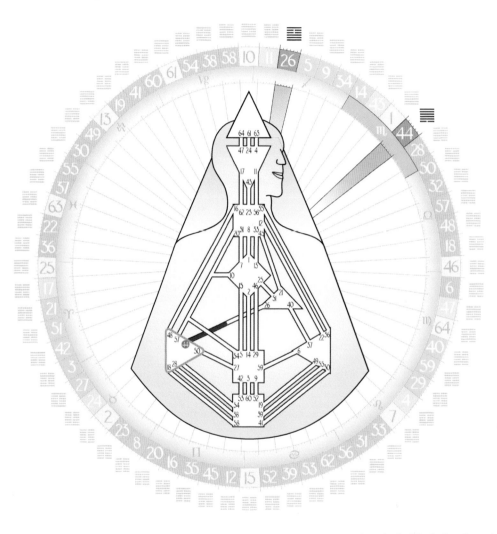

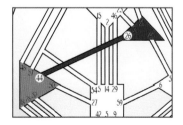

Part of Channel 26-44

The Channel of Enterprise

Center: **Spleen**   Circuit: **Tribal/ Entrepreneurial**

Astrological Period: **Scorpio** ♏

Astrological Positions:

	07°37'30" – 13°15'00" ♏
1:	07°37'30" – 08°33'45" ♏
2:	08°33'45" – 09°30'00" ♏
3:	09°30'00" – 10°26'15" ♏
4:	10°26'15" – 11°22'30" ♏
5:	11°22'30" – 12°18'45" ♏
6:	12°18'45" – 13°15'00" ♏

In all interactions there is a need to remain alert to relevant instinctive clues rather than be distracted by ego (separateness) manipulation. By 'following your nose,' you have instant access to your innate Cellular Memory that identifies how the patterns of life are interwoven.

Interference

Distrustful ◇ Misjudging : Teamwork :: Symmetry

44.1 Being Alert: Watching all internal sensations while interacting with others.
You either pay attention to your instinctive warnings or ignore them and endure the outcomes.
☽: Your vigilance gauges potential complications and rearranges them for your own benefit.
♀: If you are overly moderate towards disturbing situations you will eventually falter.

44.2 Being Conscientious: Watching any impulse to give yourself away.
When you restrain any impulses to act carelessly you can easily handle situations clearly..
♃: Your alertness to changing patterns gives you an easy tolerance in confronting anything.
♂: Your brash way of interacting may cause you to ignore your hunches and lose perspective.

44.3 Holding back: Recognizing an occasional need to hesitate in asserting yourself.
Trusting your instincts or needing to impress others, makes you clear or not in your actions.
♂: With instinctive confidence and drive you can handle tricky people and difficult situations.
♆: You often misinterpret situations and this may cause you to be confused by others' egos.

44.4 Forbearing: Finding tolerance in your interactions with others.
Being clear with your own intentions or not, allows for you ever to have anyone else's support.
☽: You have clear relations with others by engaging with them as part of your vital reality.
☉: You often assume assistance from people despite your previously being distant towards them.

44.5 Integrating: Upholding a presence that is exemplary.
You align with the laws of nature and high integrity, or take advantage if you can.
☿: Your brilliance shines through your principles and virtue, setting a a clear example for all.
♂: You have a drive to convince others in ways that maneuver them to your own advantage.

44.6 Withdrawing: Protecting yourself from becoming overwhelmed.
Distancing yourself from complex situations ensures your own well being but attracts criticism.
☽: You move through tough situations advantageously while maintaining others' support.
⊕: If you take yourself too seriously you will miss much of the fun that life offers.

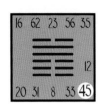

45

萫 **Gathering Together**

Rulership: (The King or Queen)

Firm alignment with that which supports everyone best brings together a strong community.

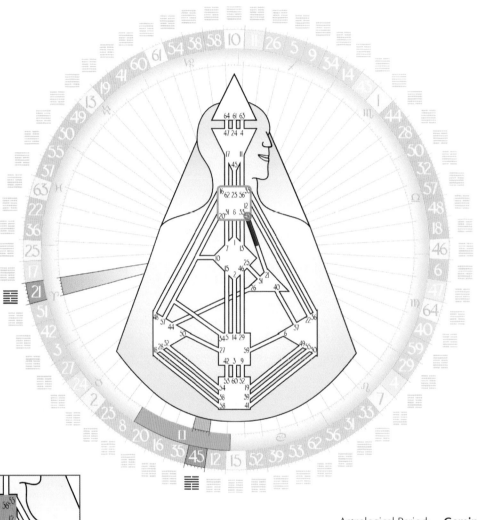

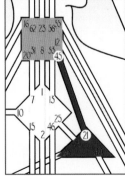

Part of Channel 21-45

The Channel of Money

Center: **Throat**   Circuit: **Tribal**

Astrological Period: **Gemini** ♊

Astrological Positions:

17°00'00" ♊ – 22°37'30" ♊

1:	17°00'00" ♊ – 17°56'15" ♊
2:	17°56'15" ♊ – 18°52'30" ♊
3:	18°52'30" ♊ – 19°48'45" ♊
4:	19°48'45" ♊ – 20°45'00" ♊
5:	20°45'00" ♊ – 21°41'15" ♊
6:	21°41'15" ♊ – 22°37'30" ♊

A stable and upright presence is required of all of those who are in positions of rulership, and so you find consensus in life through exercising your own clarity. You provide education for the wellbeing of your people. The voice of the Community relates to material fulfillment.

Dominance

Timid ⬦ Pompous : Synthesis :: Communion

45.1 Blending: Finding common ground with others before moving forwards.

Your openness and firmness in any leadership role encourages the backing of those being led.

♃: Your clear inner intent expands your ability to receive material and spiritual assistance.

♂: Being naturally attractive to others you can become overwhelmed by their problems.

45.2 Contributing: Trusting in the guidance and company you attract.

Being open or closed in the company you attract measures the blessings that you receive.

♀: Your natural attunement to your company opens the way for unexpected blessings.

♂: You tend to "go it alone" rather than appreciate the blessings that your company brings.

45.3 Separating: Proceeding in life without obvious support or common accord.

You either discover how to gather resources and support or find troubles that create hardship.

♆: Your deep attunement to the workings within a hierarchy intuits how to gain resources.

♂: Disappointed not finding common accord, you might ask : "Do I truly want to be involved?"

45.4 Being Brave: Selflessly striving to accomplish benefits for one and all.

You attract others by proceeding towards a larger than personal goal.

♃: Your inner alignment with a higher sense of purpose assists everyone on the material plane.

♂: Your boldness to achieve individual material success can also benefit other people.

45.5 Being Virtuous: The virtues that attract the confidence of others.

Your attitudes of independence or entitlement affect the way in which you are perceived.

♀: Your innovative approach to leadership is naturally attractive to other people.

♃: Assuming a grandiose approach to leading others you must be practical to be effective.

45.6 Being Self-dependent: Trusting that you receive what you need.

You remain unfazed by others' attitudes, or capitulate when challenged materially.

♀: Relying on your inner independence you succeed despite employing unorthodox techniques.

♃: Taking 'failure' personally you'll find regrets. You are reminded to count your blessings!

升 Serendipity
Self Determination
Growth and good fortune come through application, truthfulness and sincerity, or, simply by being in the right place at the right time with the right attitude.

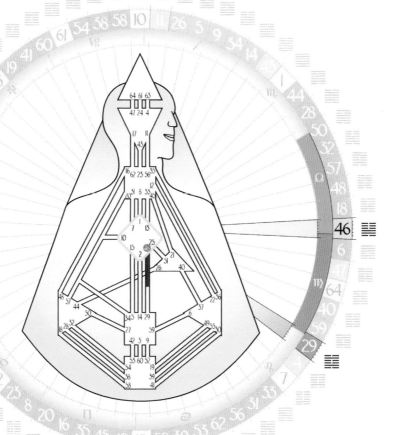

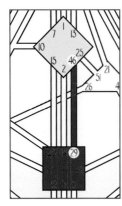

Part of Channel 29-46
The Channel of Discovery

Center: **Self**   Circuit: **Collective/Sensing**

Astrological Period: **Virgo** ♍
   Libra ♎

Astrological Positions:

	28°15'00" ♍ – 03°52'30" ♓
1:	28°15'00" ♍ – 29°11'15" ♍
2:	29°11'15" ♍ – 00°07'30" ♎
3:	00°07'30" ♎ – 01°03'45" ♎
4:	01°03'45" ♎ – 02°00'00" ♎
5:	02°00'00" ♎ – 02°56'15" ♎
6:	02°56'15" ♎ – 03°52'30" ♎

Small gains eventually lead to great accomplishments. Love of your body is love of your temple, or love of the vehicle that conveys you through your precious life.

Seriousness

Frigid ◇ Frivolous : Delight :: Ecstasy

46.1 Promoting: Inner conviction is recognized by those who seek to align with you.
Your inherent confidence or a lack of readiness to grow either attracts assistance or not.

Ψ: Your personal commitment to your life ensures you grow in both obvious and unseen ways.

♃: If you insist on developing solely by your own efforts you might miss some potential allies.

46.2 Expanding: Like it or not, the eyes are on you and you can deliver!
Even with modest resources and without others' approval you grow through just being you.

☉: Success is assured by your clear sincerity, coupled with your bright nature.

♂: Striving ambitiously for recognition and success, you may not be appreciated by others.

46.3 Progressing: Moving upwards in life without doubts.
When proceeding into the unknown, you need not hesitate so long as you are clear in yourself.

☾: You advance easily in life through your inner attunement to all phases of your journey.

♂: Finding little resistance in life you may try to advance by using unsuccessful associations.

46.4 Fulfilling: Holding true to your inner commitment to grow.
Being recognized for your commitment to grow in life allows for easy advancement.

⊕: Taking growth in your stride, you are furthered in life by receiving the trust of others.

☋: Believing growth to be part of life's process you may fail to acknowledge those who assist.

46.5 Proceeding: A naturally powerful development needs strong inner virtue.
You are growing in your journey through life whether you see visible signs of progress or not.

☾: Maintaining your balance in all phases of life allows for successful and lasting growth.

Ψ: Getting lost in imagination distracts you from a consistency that is needed for sure growth.

46.6 Re-appraising: Compulsive advancement requires constant vigilance.
Reviewing your life's efforts you determine who and what receives your energy and attention.

♄: When you always relate realistically to your life you are available to interact with others.

Ψ: Trusting only in your spiritual qualities you can be unaligned with the needs of the moment.

困 Realization

Mental Exhaustion: The "Aha! Moment."

Comprehension comes through a process of constantly filtering the contents of your mind to remove half-truths and untruths, then relaxing to allow for realization.

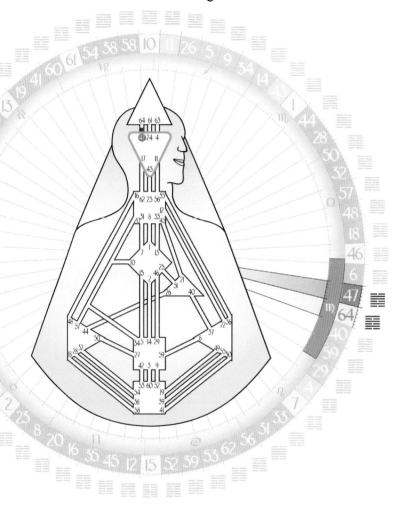

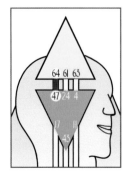

Part of Channel 64-47

The Channel of Abstract Thinking

Center: **Mind**   Circuit: **Collective/Sensing**

Astrological Period: **Virgo** ♍

Astrological Positions:

17°00'00" ♍ – 22°37'30" ♍

1:	17°00'00" ♍ – 17°56'15" ♍
2:	17°56'15" ♍ – 18°52'30" ♍
3:	18°52'30" ♍ – 19°48'45" ♍
4:	19°48'45" ♍ – 20°45'00" ♍
5:	20°45'00" ♍ – 21°41'15" ♍
6:	21°41'15" ♍ – 22°37'30" ♍

Some things make sense, some things make no sense, and some things are plainly nonsense. You examine past associations for a realization that makes a distinction. The mind has its limits...

Oppression
Hopeless ◇ Mentally oppressed : Transmutation :: Transfiguration

47 (47)

47.1 Reviewing: The Truth is constant but sometimes remains hidden from us.
By mental self-examination you remove useless beliefs or else risk feeling overwhelmed.

♄: Your meditative quality watches the mind and filters out self-defeating thought patterns.

Ψ: An unrealistic sense of hope links you to an over-reliance on the mind's grasp of life.

47.2 Being Fortunate: Aligning with resonant causes furthers your journey.
Outer disputes can easily become inner ones, unless you sidestep others' discords altogether.

♄: Inner stability keeps you apart from your mind's constant comparison mechanism.

☿: With an uncertain mind it is important you make decisions by accessing your Authority.

47.3 Being Confused: A purely mental viewpoint can be unrealistically restrictive.
Constantly thinking things are worse than they really are is an easy way to become depressed.

♃: Relaxing in deep trust in yourself and Existence allows truth to be finally revealed to you!

♂: Attempting to justify your life purpose through your thoughts fuels a deep discontentment.

47.4 Holding Focus: Maintaining your way in a confused world.
Being persistent you find your way among others' fossilized and poor views, or else you give up.

♄: Your meditative approach picks out apparently fixed agendas and obsolete belief systems.

☾: Your attunement with many diverse possible views in life can lead to personal confusion.

47.5 Endorsing: Making sense out of apparently impossible scenarios.
Remaining steadfast regardless of how situations appear at first, you bring joy and relief for all.

♀: The realization of Universal harmony that includes everyone, even your detractors.

☿: The truth will become apparent if you honor your clear principles.

47.6 Being Remorseful: A nagging sense of 'What's the point?' A call to go beyond the mind.
You cannot expect to think your way through life and live life fully at the same time.

☉: By constant self examination you realize that your mind is limited in making sense of life.

⊕ Stuck with multiple, often irrelevant considerations, you will find it hard to move on in life.

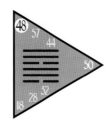

井 The Well
Freshness & Depth : Knowledge
Replenishment comes through establishing and re-establishing access to the unending source of knowledge.

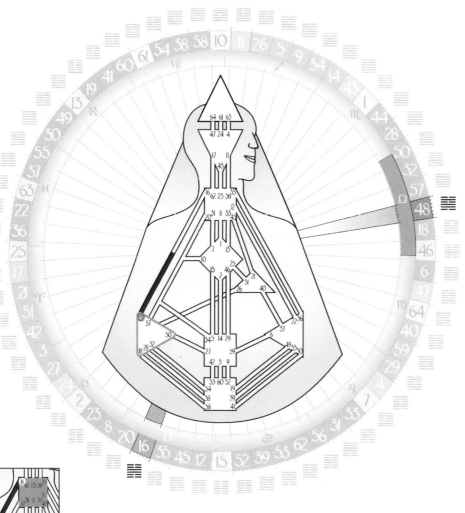

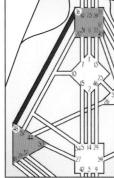

Part of Channel 16-48
The Channel of Talent

Center: **Spleen**   Circuit: **Collective/Logic**

Astrological Period: **Libra ♎**

Astrological Positions:

09°30′00″ ♎ – 15°07′30″ ♎

1:	09°30′00″ ♎ – 10°26′15″ ♎
2:	10°26′15″ ♎ – 11°22′30″ ♎
3:	11°22′30″ ♎ – 12°18′45″ ♎
4:	12°18′45″ ♎ – 13°15′00″ ♎
5:	13°15′00″ ♎ – 14°11′15″ ♎
6:	14°11′15″ ♎ – 15°07′30″ ♎

The possibility for civilization on Earth exists as we access and utilize knowledge that comes from a natural source. The well, the source of water, is the essential fresh-flowing sustenance for all of life. The sense of taste.

Inadequacy

Inadequate ◇ Thirsty : Resourcefulness :: Wisdom

48.1 Finding Significance: Quick recognition of relevance or irrelevance in your life.

You either adjust to each fresh moment or find life distasteful and become distracted.

☾: You have a natural attunement with all manner of gifts that life brings to you.

♂: Making problems out of nothing you find it hard to be satisfied with life's simple pleasures.

48.2 Deteriorating: The need to constantly refresh your gifts.

Your talents deteriorate when ignored or if you are distracted by comparing yourself to others.

♅: You transform your abilities by growing in and around the challenges that life brings.

♀: You are careless in practicing your gifts when you are distracted by other influences in your life.

48.3 Acknowledging: Trusting in your adaptable gifts.

Sooner or later you are appreciated for your talents and abilities if you trust and persevere.

☾: You have the endurance to expand your gifts so that they are appreciated by one and all.

☿: Being fearful and worried that you may be overlooked can contribute to being overlooked.

48.4 Refreshing: All your gifts benefit from regular reevaluation and refreshment.

In rest, refreshment and reevaluation your inner depth and clarity are explored and expanded.

☉: You put your own life in order as a priority, ready for openings to extend into others' lives.

⊕: You tend to over-identify with projects that exhaust you when they hit snags.

48.5 Utilizing: Recognizing that you have many gifts, but also the need to apply them.

Using your abilities towards great benefits requires that you remain clear to each moment.

♂: By savoring each moment, you appreciate the gifts that most easily benefit everyone.

☾: If you question your own gifts and adopt others' ways, you'll be unfulfilled by your deeds.

48.6 Replenishing: Fulfillment comes through sharing from an overflowing source.

Great fulfillment comes from the openness to share your extensive gifts with others.

♀: Harmonizing your world through sharing your source of understandings and talents.

☾: Moodiness and uncertainty can cause you to be coaxed by other people to share your gifts.

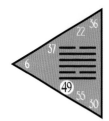

革 Revolution
Principles : The Rebel
Emotion abolishes the 'old' in the interest of supporting a 'new' that is aligned with particular principles.

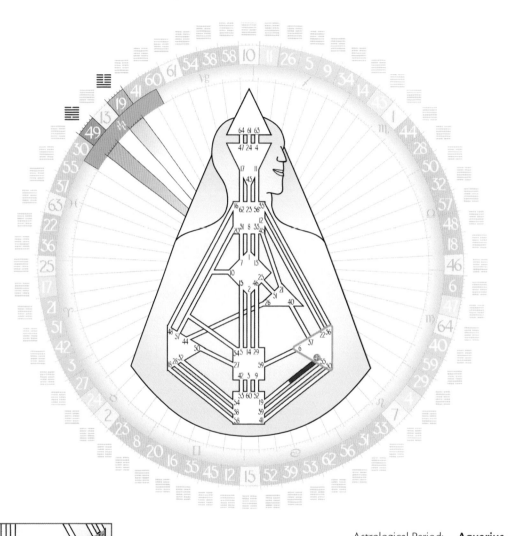

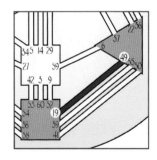

Part of Channel 19-49
Channel of Sensitivity

Center: **Emotions**　　Circuit: **Tribal/Community**

Astrological Period:　**Aquarius** ♒

Astrological Positions:

	18°52'30" ♒ – 24°30'00" ♒
1:	18°52'30" ♒ – 19°48'15" ♒
2:	19°48'45" ♒ – 20°45'30" ♒
3:	20°45'00" ♒ – 21°41'45" ♒
4:	21°41'15" ♒ – 22°37'00" ♒
5:	22°37'30" ♒ – 23°33'15" ♒
6:	23°33'45" ♒ – 24°30'00" ♒

Any revolution brings a wave of change that must be timed rightly and be felt to be practical to have lasting merit. A "No!" "Reaction" evolves to "Revolution" evolves to "The Rebel."
Gate 49 is a transpecial bridge that attunes with mammals.
Reaction
Inert ⬦ Rejecting/Reactive : Revolution :: Rebirth

49.1 Awaiting Right Timing: Conserving your energy until you have clarity.

Noticing many changing potentials you have the awareness to wait for right circumstances.

♃: Your honorable behavior in every all situation fosters your growth.

☉: Inducing idealistic changes can cause you to be continually justifying yourself.

49.2 Being Firm: Envisioning right outcomes for changes.

Recognizing that change is needed, you either hold to firm principles or act for change's sake.

⊕: Your grounded disposition holds you in your principles when times of change come.

☽: Chaotic circumstances can cause you to overturn everything that appears already resolved.

49.3 Informing: Finding the support of other people in times of change.

In times of upheaval there needs to be mutual agreement for everyone to be ready for changes.

♆: Your sensitivity relates to the principles of change and informs others of what is happening.

☽: Getting caught up in the drama of change you become insensitive to the needs of others.

49.4 Making Ready: Accumulating energy and motivation for radical changes.

Sincerely aligning with your truth, or simply being opportunistic, you enrich or deplete society.

♃: Your expanded overview of society's needs allows you to implement changes that benefit all.

♂: Your forceful nature can take advantage over others during times of upheaval.

49.5 Being Sentient: The inner feeling for the rightness of changes.

Seeing a need for change, you support others with their approval or in order to control them.

☾: You align everyone in ways that make it easier to transition through upheavals.

♂: Your impatience with others can drive you to attempt to force change on them.

49.6 Appreciating: Content to expand on previous changes.

With all changes, further growth is possible when everyone adjusts to the new circumstances.

♆: Appreciating yourself and others supports everyone to drop the old and grow with the new.

♄: If you seek perfection in transitioning situations it can be hard for others to feel appreciated.

50

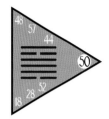

鼎 Values
Stability
Honoring the wisdom and being responsible for values that enrich both local community and society at large.

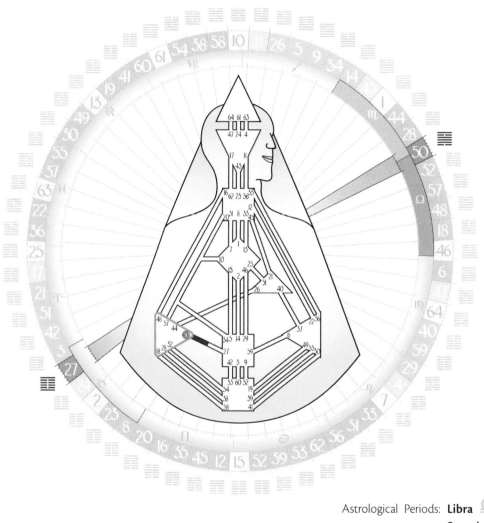

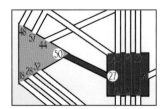

Part of Channel 27-50
The Channel of Preservation

Center: **Spleen**   Circuit: **Tribal/Defense**

Astrological Periods: **Libra** ♎︎
                       Scorpio ♏︎

Astrological Positions:

26°22'30" ♎︎ – 02°00'00" ♏︎

1:	26°22'30" ♎︎ – 27°18'45" ♎︎
2:	27°18'45" ♎︎ – 28°15'00" ♎︎
3:	28°15'00" ♎︎ – 29°11'15" ♎︎
4:	29°11'15" ♎︎ – 00°07'30" ♏︎
5:	00°07'30" ♏︎ – 01°03'45" ♏︎
6:	01°03'45" ♏︎ – 02°00'00" ♏︎

Spiritual and Earthly powers are joined by taking responsibility to hold and promote values of merit that are traditional or novel, but which are relevant to the essential needs of any instance.

Corruption

Irresponsible ⬦ Overloaded : Equilibrium :: Harmony

50.1 Starting Afresh: Eliminating old qualities before honoring new ones.
Being clear that adopted values may no longer be appropriate in your life and community.
♂: The drive for refinement compels you to use any means to achieve your ends.
♀: Dissatisfaction with all your original values, opens a tendency to borrow others' values.

50.2 Standing firm: Avoiding tempting distractions from your natural way.
Being firm in your values or giving in to outside pressures, you always accept the consequences.
☉: Being strong to uphold your values mirrors your inner calm no matter how others react.
♀: When confronted by others' values you tend to be self-defensive, and easily compromised.

50.3 Clarifying: Be clear that you recognize and honor your own true values first.
Honoring your own values you receive the support you need, but may regret being assisted.
☽: Being aware that you require support, you establish the values needed to receive it.
☿: You might be overly mental in balancing your values with your need for acceptance.

50.4 Qualifying: Presence is needed in upholding right values in sorry circumstances.
In all situations, values need to correspond to the real requirements of the present moment.
♄: A meditative quality ensures your values are in accord with the needs of every occasion.
♂: Your drive to expound unformed values to achieve a result can cause chaos

50.5 Enhancing: Maintaining alertness to recognize which values serve best.
You recognize or disregard a correlation between the values and actions that serve everyone.
♄: You grow wise enough to uphold appropriate values when pressured to change them.
♂: In a rush to get on in life, you can disregard the real values that serve yourself and others.

50.6 Invigorating: Consistently supporting the values that serve one and all.
You set an example with clarity and wisdom, whether you relate closely with others or not.
♀: The strength of your inner harmony compels others to realize the essential values in life.
☽: Your occasionally moody nature can allow your clarity to become obscured by trifles.

51

震 **Arousing**
Shock : Gall
Individual initiative acts in relation to disruption, rearrangement and drastic changes.

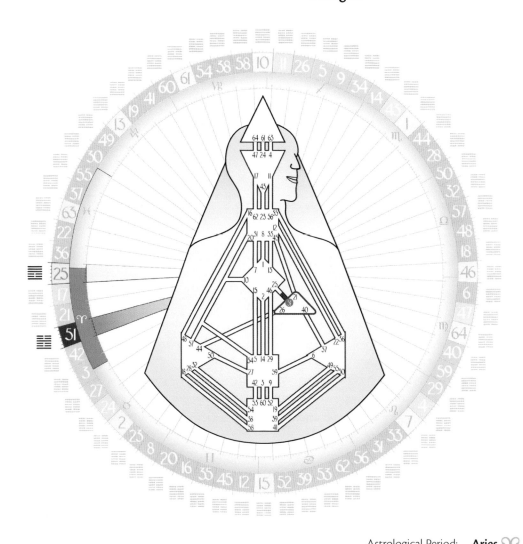

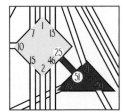

Part of Channel 25-51
The Channel of Initiation

Center: **Heart**   Circuit: **Individual/ Centering**

Astrological Period: **Aries** ♈

Astrological Positions:

	15°07'30" ♈ – 20°45'00" ♈
1:	15°07'30" ♈ – 16°03'45" ♈
2:	16°03'45" ♈ – 17°00'00" ♈
3:	17°00'00" ♈ – 17°56'15" ♈
4:	17°56'15" ♈ – 18°52'30" ♈
5:	18°52'30" ♈ – 19°48'45" ♈
6:	19°48'45" ♈ – 20°45'00" ♈

Thunder is the shock wave that rattles the heavens, and shakes us awake. It wakens us to appreciate there are sometimes forgotten forces at play, and alternative possibilities in life that can be tried. A bolt out of the blue makes it possible in any moment, to transcend ego-separation and jump into a personally truthful reality.

Agitation

Cowardly $\diamondsuit$ Agitated : Initiative :: Awakening

51.1 Arousing: Growing through disruptions of all kinds.

Dramatic change can be alarming until you accept all of the transformations it brings.

☾: Transformation is your nature and you find a relative ease adapting to dramatic situations.

♀: You are very sensitive to shocks and the upsets they bring, often wishing to avoid them.

51.2 Surviving: Recognizing temporary upsets for what they are : temporary.

Everything comes around, and if you wait patiently, you transcend shock and apparent defeat.

♂: You confidently take well-timed, evasive action in overwhelming situations.

☿: Mental indecision will often cause you to miss the right time to act in shocking situations.

51.3 Being Composed: Learning to honor the laws of nature.

In times of shock you either grow through calmly realigning with the inherent changes, or not.

☉: The power to deal with disruption is linked to your ability to calmly find a way through it.

♃: You may take shocks as a personal affront to your ego that compels you to struggle with life.

51.4 Being Unstructured: Beyond habitual reactions....... "Going outside the box."

Dramatic times bring opportunities that you either grasp or fumble.

♁: Your spiritual warrior is thrilled by shocking events and takes on all challenges.

☿: Trying to master intense drama and shock with your mental programs can cause chaos.

51.5 Being Reliable: Accepting all the changes that repeated shocks bring.

You reach your goals by following your inner guidance through all manner of disruptions.

☉: You have the inner strength to find your own and others' truth in all extreme situations.

♂: You may become so engaged with fixing disruptions that you lose track of your journey.

51.6 Regenerating: The phoenix rises from the ashes anew.

Shock brings you dramatic shifts from old accords, beliefs and understandings to new ones.

☉: Your nature is to endure, grow and even flourish through all forms of intense challenges.

☾: You identify with great disruptions and disasters, often in life or death circumstances.

52

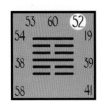

良 **Mountain**
Keeping Still
Your inner stillness and quietness
allows you to gain perspective over
all life's circumstances.

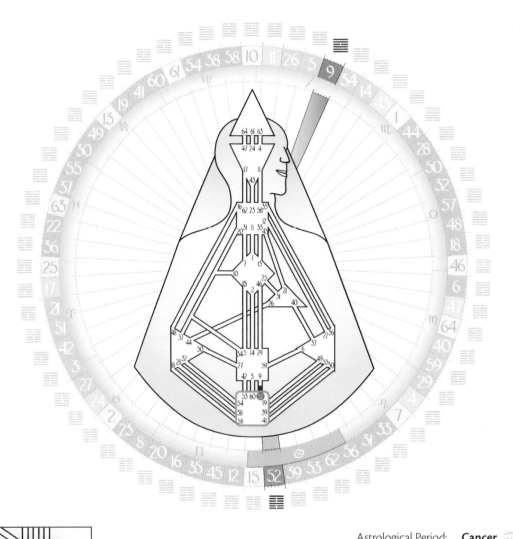

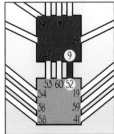

Part of Channel 9-52
The Channel of Concentration

Center: **Root** Circuit: **Collective/Logic**

Astrological Period: **Cancer** ♋

Astrological Positions:

03°52'30" ♋ – 09°30'00" ♋

1:	03°52'30" ♋ – 04°48'15" ♋
2:	04°48'45" ♋ – 05°45'30" ♋
3:	05°45'00" ♋ – 06°41'45" ♋
4:	06°41'15" ♋ – 07°37'00" ♋
5:	07°37'30" ♋ – 08°33'15" ♋
6:	08°33'45" ♋ – 09°30'00" ♋

The mountain stands serene, contemplating the commotion in the valleys below, and offering a calming presence...witnessing it all. Meditation leads to health and wholeness in your journey through life.
From the Mountaintop, enjoy the view!

Stress
Stuck ⬦ Restless : Restraint :: Stillness

52.1 Pause before acting: Inner stillness is sufficient unto itself.
Your firmness to always act appropriately or anxiety to act anyhow, affects everything in life.

⊕: At ease in life, you are able to pause for personal reflection before doing anything.

♂: Your restlessness has difficulty in waiting, and often commits you to unrealistic causes.

52.2 Be still and know: Releasing fears and concerns around your apparent inaction.
When attracted by outside influences it is important to remain true to your own way.

♀: You pause for clarity in which you see your outer reality as a reflection of your inner being.

♂: You can easily get swept up in all manner of events that do not serve you entirely.

52.3 Being Resigned: Inner composure in times when nothing needs to happen.
You resist acting to accumulate unnecessary resources, or become pressured and resentful.

♄: Your meditative nature allows you to pause to recoup your energy and review your purpose.

♀: Pressured into attempting to find harmony in restrictive circumstances, you'll find little.

52.4 Keeping Still: Avoiding strong urges to act just to combat restlessness.
You avoid reckless actions through self-mastery, or tend to be frustrated when inactive.

♄: You embrace self-mastery and personal freedom through meditation and gentle restraint.

♃: Doubting your purpose during times of inaction, you tend to try to make yourself busy.

52.5 Being Attentive: Words and actions are not necessarily the same thing.
Being careful giving guidance or getting muddled between what you say and what gets done.

⊕: You are at ease in being reliable for what you say, and how, why and when action is needed.

☽: Outspoken comments bring transformation but also regrets when you are misunderstood.

52.6 Meaning: Finding clarity in your inner stillness.
Your calm appreciation comes through an inner stability unaffected by all outside pressures.

♀: Inner development brings the tranquility that allows you to meld into the mysteries of life.

♆: Your imaginative quality enters into the core of stillness and rests apart from the world.

53

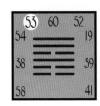

 New Beginnings
Development
Gradual advance takes place as an organic process that brings increasing self-knowledge and experience.

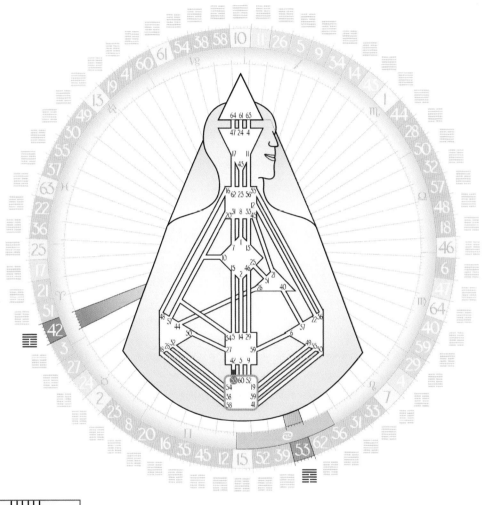

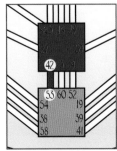

Part of Channel 42-53
The Channel of Cycles

Center: **Root**   Circuit: **Collective/Sensing**

Astrological Period: **Cancer** ♋
Astrological Positions:

15°07'30" ♋ – 20°45'00" ♋

1:    15°07'30" ♋ – 16°03'45" ♋
2:    16°03'45" ♋ – 17°00'00" ♋
3:    17°00'00" ♋ – 17°56'15" ♋
4:    17°56'15" ♋ – 18°52'30" ♋
5:    18°52'30" ♋ – 19°48'45" ♋
6:    19°48'45" ♋ – 20°45'00" ♋

You sense the pressure to commence something... anything, so long as it is new and different from what has been experienced before. The phenomenon of being drawn into experiences and projects of all sorts without much consideration of completion......

Immaturity

Fickle ◇ Staid : Expansion :: Superabundance

53

53.1 Commencing: Great progress comes from well-considered beginnings.
You grow in life by refining your abilities to start new ventures.

Ψ: Holding your vision and relying on your own strengths you grow in new life experiences.

♀: Being vulnerable to criticism from those you wish to impress dampens your development.

53.2 Fortune Smiles: The sense of security in your growth.
Growth can be easy and shared as long as you remain alert to your own inner guidance.

☾: A centered and expanding growth comes easily in all aspects of your life.

♂: Careless in your inner attitude you easily succumb to the pressures of unbridled growth.

53.3 Scrutinizing: Watching your step when engaging in all new endeavors.
Be clear that you cannot always predict the effects that your developments have on others.

☾: Finding growth potential in all situations you draw from your inner strengths.

♂: You have a potential to dissipate your energy fighting with life rather than growing in life.

53.4 Being Agile: Finding your balance in all new situations.
When proceeding under pressure you rely on your inner stability, or succumb to stress.

☾: Your inner calm preserves your growth through any difficult circumstance.

♀: Pressured by the expectations of others you seek personal growth in novel situations.

53.5 Advancing Steadily: In all expansion you are going to be pressured from outside.
You stay true to your own measure of growth or become overwhelmed by life's pressures.

Ψ: Your deep attunement to growth comes by adapting in your own way to any situation.

⊕: Becoming overly identified with a process can insulate you from your own natural growth.

53.6 Bringing Benefit: The endless and natural gift of service to others.
In your own growth, you emanate service and example that spreads to others' lives.

☾: You remain true to your own path of growth and live as a shining example for others.

♅: Embracing transformation and growth you don't always recognize how that affects others.

54

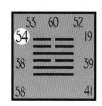

歸妹 Ambition

Both material and spiritual
Proceeding in life through committing first to your independence, and then to outside sources that can assist.

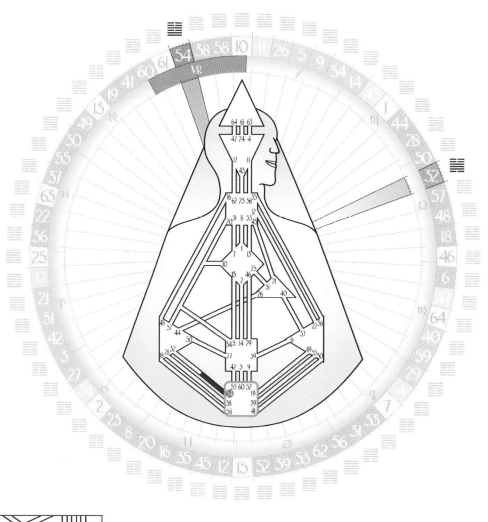

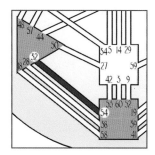

Part of Channel 32-54
The Channel of Transformation

Center: **Root**   Circuit: **Tribal/Entrepreneurial**

Astrological Period: **Capricorn** ♑
Astrological Positions:

15°07'30" ♑ – 20°45'00" ♑

1:	15°07'30" ♑ – 16°03'45" ♑
2:	16°03'45" ♑ – 17°00'00" ♑
3:	17°00'00" ♑ – 17°56'15" ♑
4:	17°56'15" ♑ – 18°52'30" ♑
5:	18°52'30" ♑ – 19°48'45" ♑
6:	19°48'45" ♑ – 20°45'00" ♑

Maintaining your balance in what often turns out to be subordinate and even demeaning situations, allows you to align with your own guidance that directs you to your own strength and ways to advance.

Greed

Indifferent ◇ Greedy : Aspiration :: Ascension

54.1 Being Confident: Even in lowly situations, be true to yourself.
You complete everything in your life by associating with those who lend their support.

(◉): You grow in life, regardless of perceived limitations, because of your many associations.

♀: Seeking 'politically correct' associations rather than those that may actually assist you.

54.2 Resolving: Holding firmly to your vision of transformation.
Having a clear perception of what you consider 'right,' or feeling entitled to special assistance.

♄: It is important you maintain the quality of your interactions with those who assist you.

♂: Your occasional recklessness can make you take advantage of influential people in your life.

54.3 Being Prudent: Compromising yourself is possible through indiscretions.
You patiently avoid shortcuts to transformation or grasp every chance and find great trials.

(◉): Employing many different alliances to proceed in life you move through your limitations.

♀: You compromise yourself through relationships with anyone who might advance you in life.

54.4 Illuminating: Acknowledging that Existence has Her plans for us.
Transformation in its purest form, when you realize that what you want is not necessarily worth having, and then finding how to live with that. You find equanimity and the balance between the Earth and Spirit Planes. (Each planet has its own particular interface in this line.)

54.5 Finding Spirituality: Holding high principles in all aspects of your life.
You are available to assist the needs of the moment and maintain stability for transformation.

☉: With your bright nature you go out of your way to ensure that what is necessary happens.

⊕ If you overly identify with mundane aspects of life you limit your potential transformation.

54.6 Being Politically Correct: Watchful of your purpose and sincerity.
Energizing those interactions that are essential, or just being seen to 'do the right thing.'

♄: Being honest in your motives you stick to respectfully advantageous relationships.

♃: Wasting energy in 'doing the right thing' you concede that that transformation is unlikely.

55

豐 **Abundance**
Spirit
A spirited nature is not reasonable but
has the means to access abundance
in all manners of expression.

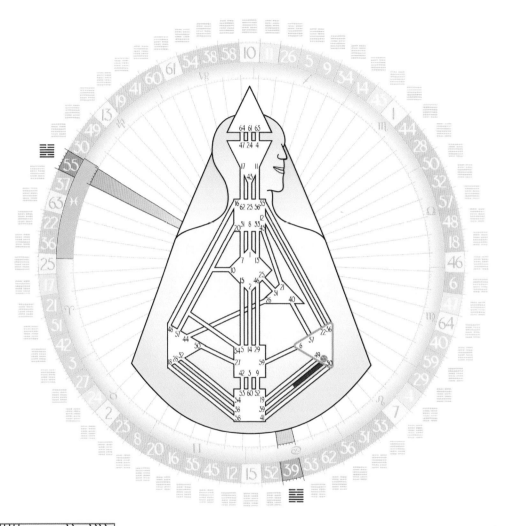

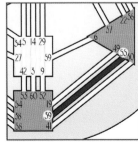

Part of Channel 39-55
The Channel of Emoting

Center: **Emotions**   Circuit: **Individual/**
                                              Knowing

Astrological Period: **Pisces** ⟩(

Astrological Positions:

	00°07'30" ⟩(– 05°45'00" ⟩(
1:	00°07'30" ⟩(– 01°03'45" ⟩(
2:	01°03'45" ⟩(– 02°00'00" ⟩(
3:	02°00'00" ⟩(– 02°56'15" ⟩(
4:	02°56'15" ⟩(– 03°52'30" ⟩(
5:	03°52'30" ⟩(– 04°48'45" ⟩(
6:	04°48'45" ⟩(– 05°45'00" ⟩(

Sometimes dramatic waves of spirited emotions move through you without any rational rhyme or reason. An emotional trigger to Creativity involves knowing both melancholy and bliss.

Victimization

Victimized ◇ Complaining : Freedom :: FREEDOM!

55.1 Relating: Being open and available to those of like mind and sentiment.

You connect to others on a similar wavelength or seek out company for purely social reasons.

♃: You promote abundance through aligning yourself with those of similar disposition.

♀: You align with others out of a concern for sociability rather than for mutuality.

55.2 Remaining Innocent: Holding your own when surrounded by skepticism.

You provoke suspicion in others through your ideals and can be coerced by their mistrust.

♀: Trusting your senses you align with those who live in accord with your own reality.

⊕: Identifying with being considered trustworthy you are deeply shaken when challenged.

55.3 Eclipsing: Being your best in challenging circumstances.

You find patience and your strength of Spirit when halted, or else you feel compelled to react.

♄: You have the emotional discipline to survive failures without taking them too personally.

♂: You can feel failure as a personal insult and do anything to protect your deflated spirit.

55.4 Brightening: Your inner wisdom shines out for other people in difficult times.

You find those who truly value your spirit, and either make wise decisions, or take chances.

♃: Your spirited nature aligns with others in making wise decisions that bring great abundance.

♂: Attracting others with your spirited nature you easily rush your decisions and cause upsets.

55.5 Counseling: Being quite clear in the companions you have.

Your inner harmony guarantees a magnanimous spirit and abundance for yourself and others.

☊: Innovative in applying your ideals and the counsels of others, you provide great abundance.

☉: Engaging the counsels of others intelligently but maybe feeling conditioned and restrained.

55.6 Being Selfless: Holding open views and much allowance for your world.

It is easy to abandon those less fortunate than yourself if you are not watchful.

♄: You have the discipline to use your abundance to further the lives of yourself and others.

☾: If you take yourself too seriously you will miss much of the fun that life offers.

56

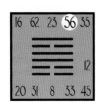

旅 The Wanderer
Stimulation : Traveling
The movements and views of the inner world are reflected by movements and views in the outer world.

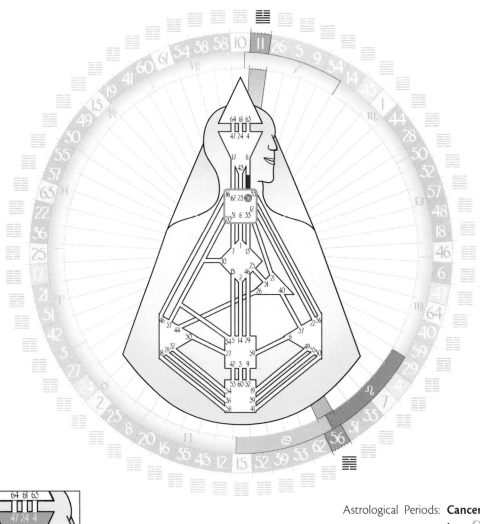

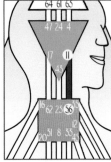

Part of Channel 11-56
The Channel of Curiosity

Center: **Throat**   Circuit: **Collective/Sensing**

Astrological Periods: **Cancer** ♋
                      Leo ♌

Astrological Positions:

26º22'30" ♋ – 02º00'00" ♌

1:	26º22'30" ♋	– 27º18'45" ♋
2:	27º18'45" ♋	– 28º15'00" ♋
3:	28º15'00" ♋	– 29º11'15" ♋
4:	29º11'15" ♋	– 00º07'30" ♌
5:	00º07'30" ♌	– 01º03'45" ♌
6:	01º03'45" ♌	– 02º00'00" ♌

Through storytelling and engaging with life as a means of testing human experiences you exercise your viewpoints and open new cycles.
The "circle of life" has the potential to become the "spiral of life" through expansive beliefs, and how they are practiced and absorbed.
Distraction
Sullen ⬦ Over-stimulated : Enrichment :: Intoxication

56

56.1 Being Intentional: Avoiding being distracted and sailing through life.

Being purposefully engaged in your life or not, qualifies the value of all of your life experiences.

☾: Relating in your own way, in your own time, to matters of personal interest.

♂: Your speech can be mostly escapist to avoid any personal responsibility for what is said.

56.2 Welcoming: The gift of enhancing your world if you trust in yourself.

Attentive to the brightness in your world, you notice how life is perceived by others.

☊: Relating innovatively in your life brings admiration and assistance in times of need.

☾: Your passion for storytelling can miss the needs and expectations of your audience.

56.3 Being Thorough: Examining any and all fixed beliefs.

You examine and update your beliefs, or you are careless how you associate them into your life.

☉: You express your beliefs with conviction and you have an ability to adjust them over time.

♀: If you believe that your true harmony exists somewhere else, you will always be restless.

56.4 Measuring: Aligning your beliefs in the context of your life journey.

You are alert to when and what you say and must be ready to talk your way out of trouble.

☾: Your sensitivity to the mood of the moment indicates what can be easily communicated.

☿: Your confusion over what needs expressing can make it hard to assert yourself effectively.

56.5 Storytelling: Drawing people to your tales and adventures.

You are crystal clear in how you relate ideas of worth, or become vain and lose your way.

☊: Finding an easy accord with others through your innovative abilities and descriptions.

♂: Your provocative manner demands expression and may relate a sense of unease to others.

56.6 Re-examining: Assessing the boundaries of what is truthful.

Your beliefs shape your perception of reality, bringing a certain quality of experiences.

☉: You experience and speak out about your inner beliefs as your constantly shifting reality.

☋: Uncomfortable with any consistent beliefs you will deliberately confuse them.

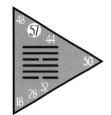

57

巽 **The Gentle**
Intuition (The Penetrating Wind)
You proceed gently while paying
attention to your intuitive clarity.

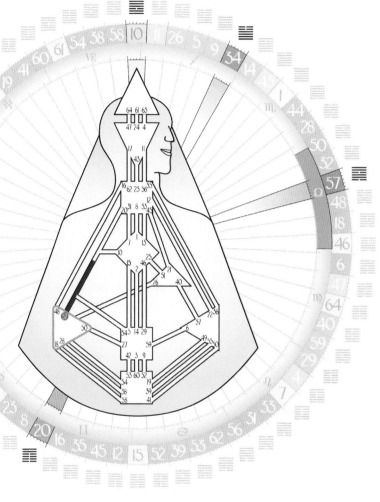

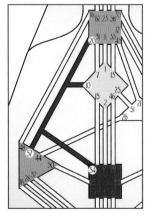

Part of Channel 10-57
The Channel of Survival

Part of Channel 20-57
The Channel of Involuntary Impulses

Part of Channel 34-57
The Channel of Power

Center: **Spleen**   Circuit: **Individual/ Knowing**

Astrological Period: **Libra** ♎

Astrological Positions:

15°07'30" ♎ – 20°45'00" ♎

1:	15°07'30" ♎ – 16°03'45" ♎
2:	16°03'45" ♎ – 17°00'00" ♎
3:	17°00'00" ♎ – 17°56'15" ♎
4:	17°56'15" ♎ – 18°52'30" ♎
5:	18°52'30" ♎ – 19°48'45" ♎
6:	19°48'45" ♎ – 20°45'00" ♎

You have access to an acoustic, vibrational sensibility that cuts through all manner of distractions to ascertain truth. Exercising intuition is literally to "teach yourself, inside yourself, according to what you hear (intuit)."

Unease

Hesitant $\diamond$ Impetuous : Intuition :: Clairaudience

57.1 Remaining Calm: The biggest fuss usually hides the silliest things.

You allow your intuition to penetrate through confusion, or become overwhelmed by chaos.

♀: You perceive upsets to your sense of acoustic harmony without being distracted.

☾: You can be upset by chaotic situations, lose your intuitive ability and become indecisive.

57.2 Infiltrating: Recognizing hidden agendas.

Your intuition penetrates to meanings hidden from other senses, giving you to act nobly or not.

♀ Your harmonic nature enriches your clarity and virtue as a matter of course.

☾: Your moodiness allows you to ignore any intuitive recognition of your baser motives.

57.3 Being Aware: Sensitive vibrational attunement.

Finding yourself immersed, even frozen sometimes in pure awareness.

☿: You have the ability to attune to and relate to your perceptions of life from a pure intuition.

♆: Your deep intuitive gift sometimes takes you beyond reality and into fantasy.

57.4 Being Fearless: Clear intuition sees afar and must not succumb to fears.

You attune deeply into your own and others' lives through considering everybody's needs.

♀: You intuit and aligning to everyone's ways and wants even before they are aware of them.

♂: You act rashly on your intuitions in directing others, sometimes treading on people's toes.

57.5 Being Gentle: Attuning to life's situations moment by moment.

You deliberately evaluate your intuition or forge ahead regardless and deal with the results.

☋: You always recognize a direct connection between transformation and trusting intuition.

☾: Your moodiness can be overwhelmed by events causing you to overlook intuitive updates.

57.6 Being Circumspect: Curbing the intuition to relevant issues that are at hand.

Your either have self-confidence or not, to trust in, and act on, what your intuition tells you.

☌: Your have an unusual gift of intuiting things that cannot be discerned by other means.

♂: Your drive to act rashly comes from a fear that you are helpless to solve difficult situations.

58

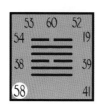

兌 **Joyous Vitality**
The Vital Spark
Appreciating the great power and
delight to have Joy in life.

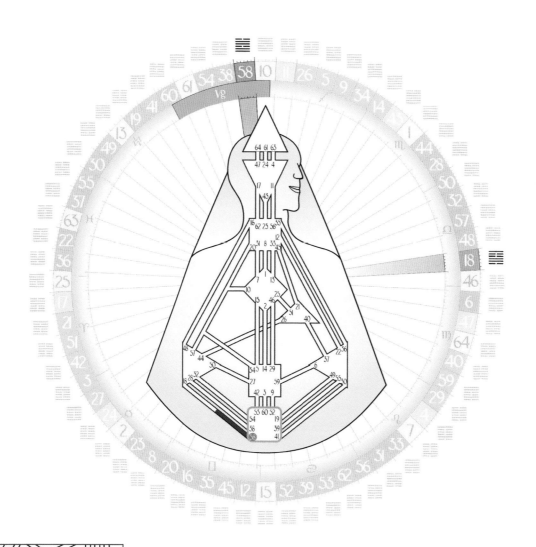

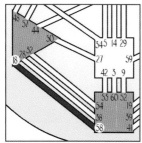

Part of Channel 18-58
The Channel of Judgement
Center: **Root**   Circuit: **Collective/Logic**

Astrological Period: **Capricorn** ♑

Astrological Positions:

03°52'30" ♑ – 09°30'00" ♑

1:	03°52'30" ♑ – 04°48'15" ♑
2:	04°48'45" ♑ – 05°45'30" ♑
3:	05°45'00" ♑ – 06°41'45" ♑
4:	06°41'15" ♑ – 07°37'00" ♑
5:	07°37'30" ♑ – 08°33'15" ♑
6:	08°33'45" ♑ – 09°30'00" ♑

At the root of all growth and endeavor enters the vital spark of life that can be described as joyfulness. In all of life's affairs, joyfulness exists in helping us find our subtle independent urge to get involved with life.

Dissatisfaction
Joyless ⬦ Interfering : Vitality :: Bliss

58.1 Harmonizing: Aligning your life with your spontaneous cheerful nature.
By living in freedom from doubts and concerns you bring joy to yourself and others.

♀: When you access your inner harmony you promote joy for one and all.

☾: Your changeable moods cycle through joy and sorrow quite naturally.

58.2 Looking Onwards: Attunement to your inner joy attracts enjoyable activities.
Your inner calm creates external joy, or you may just seek out thrills as a means to escape.

♀: You relish a harmonic balance between internal joy and external stimulations.

☋: Attracting the unusual you easily find activities that can lack apparently lasting values.

58.3 Exciting: The draw of worldly enjoyments requires great inner selectivity.
Intense excitement exists within you or is reflected through a promise of worldly pleasures.

☋: Your innovative nature can give you great diversions that electrify your very core.

♂: Restless and fascinated by worldly delights you race from one distraction to another.

58.4 Being Spontaneous: Quick recognition of joyful stimulations.
You find strictly beneficial incentives or indulge everything and become drained of energy.

⚷: You are at home in diverse and dramatic circumstances identifying what really serves you.

♆: You may get lost in which stimulations to select and make choices that exhaust you.

58.5 Being Discrete: Being clear in your inner needs and wants.
You are either clear in your associations or tend to trust everyone and end up being misled.

☾: Your openness to others is tempered by your facility to watch out for yourself at all times.

☉: Your bright nature trusts everyone openly and is let down regularly if you are not careful.

58.6 Attracting: Drawing to yourself all manner of stimulations.
Being caught up in outer distractions as a way of life you are subjected to the whims of others.

☾: If you link your inner world to outer stimulations you do not lose track of your own joy.

☿: The thrill of excitement is so strong that you can get lost in it and become wildly active.

59

渙 Intimacy
Dispersion : Genetic Strategy : Sexuality
Dissolving barriers we establish union.

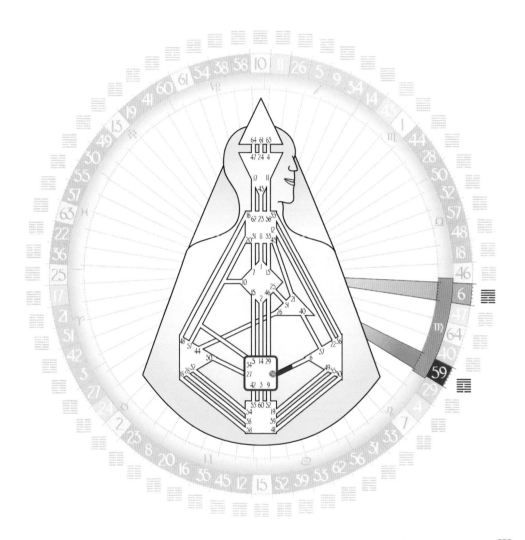

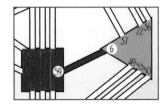

Part of Channel 59-6
The Channel of Connecting

Center: **Sacral**   Circuit: **Tribal/Defense**

Astrological Period: **Virgo** ♍

Astrological Positions:

00°07'30" ♍ – 05°45'00" ♍

1:	00°07'30" ♍ – 01°03'45" ♍
2:	01°03'45" ♍ – 02°00'00" ♍
3:	02°00'00" ♍ – 02°56'15" ♍
4:	02°56'15" ♍ – 03°52'30" ♍
5:	03°52'30" ♍ – 04°48'45" ♍
6:	04°48'45" ♍ – 05°45'00" ♍

Connecting through genetically ordered interactions allows for intimacy, openness and associations on the most profound levels in all areas of life. We all come into the world from being conceived through human intimacy, and are either willing or unwilling to acknowledge this. The sacral links us to the sacred.

Dishonesty
Excluded ◇ Intrusive : Intimacy :: Transparency

59.1 Penetrating: Evolution is only possible through interaction.
You respond decisively to openings for interaction, or hesitate and miss your chance.

☉: Your bright nature carries you through any doorway to intimacy.

☿: Finding complications in intimacy you become uncertain about when and how to interact.

59.2 Joining in: An inner separation that can also open up to profound intimacies.
Your inherent tendency to be separate eventually finds a way to be easy interrelating.

☋: Your innovative, even unusual approach to intimacy assists others to evolve in their lives.

☊: Your deeply self-involved nature can often keep others at arm's length.

59.3 Connecting: Serving yourself and your world by triggering interactions.
You are open to respond to all kinds of associations and intimacies.

♄: The sensible nature to find intimacy as a refreshment for your spirit.

♂: Actively seeking union and intimacy in any situation, sometimes being promiscuous.

59.4 Being Friendly: An openness to being friendly with anyone.
Your intimacy is founded in friendships that may become more and less intense over time.

♀: You promote friendships that dissolve established barriers and transcend tradition.

☿: Confusing your intimacy roles you risk moving into needlessly intense involvements.

59.5 Unifying: The gift of enlivening all interactions.
Relating to the needs of others, you enhance intimacy through love, respect and sexuality.

☉: You have the intense power to encourage everyone to find common accord and union.

☋: You innovatively dissolve intimacy barriers in yourself and others.

59.6 Being Discerning: You are very particular in your intimacies.
You develop a sense, over time, of how, what, when and who suits you in your intimate life.

♀: You find an inner recognition of the harmony you need to be intimately fulfilled.

☿: You find one reason or another to limit yourself in realizing profound intimacy.

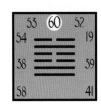

節 Limitation

Restriction : Acceptance

Accepting restrictions allows for the possibility of flow and transcendence, and the means to find new ways to re-solve (old) problems.

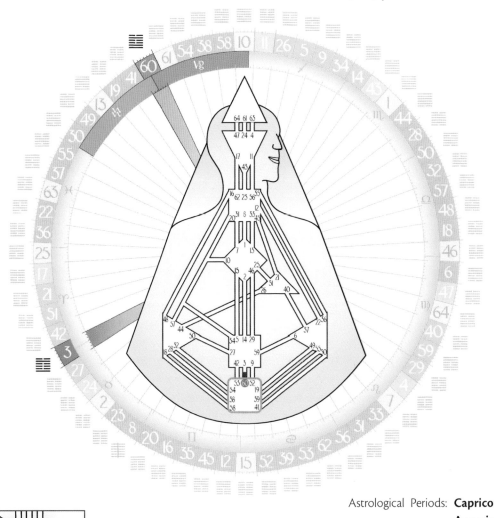

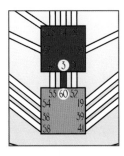

Part of Channel 3-60

The Channel of Mutation

Center: **Root**　　Circuit: **Individual/ Knowing**

Astrological Periods: **Capricorn** ♑
　　　　　　　　　　　　　Aquarius ♒

Astrological Positions:

26°22'30" ♑ – 02°00'00" ♒

1:	26°22'30" ♑ – 27°18'45" ♑
2:	27°18'45" ♑ – 28°15'00" ♑
3:	28°15'00" ♑ – 29°11'15" ♑
4:	29°11'15" ♑ – 00°07'30" ♒
5:	00°07'30" ♒ – 01°03'45" ♒
6:	01°03'45" ♒ – 02°00'00" ♒

Setting and establishing prescribed boundaries and limits provides for a known foundation from which growth and evolution can take place. When you acknowledge and take care of any restriction it becomes a potential springboard for advancement.

Limitation

Unstructured ◇ Rigid : Realism :: Justice

60.1 Accommodating: Trusting in your own dignity when under pressure.

You conserve your strength and options when confronted by restraints, or become unsettled.

♀: Your inner harmony recognizes the advantages of staying within self-imposed boundaries.

☿: You become restless and tense when you exaggerate your concerns with external restraints.

60.2 Finding Advantage: Knowing when restraints are unnecessarily limiting.

You either seize the moment to act, or feel hopelessly held back and unable to move freely.

♄: Your disciplined nature can adapt to restraints and still be ready to act.

⊕: You identify with restraints to the point that you become indecisive and immobilized.

60.3 Being Self-indulgent: Learning through exceeding your own sensible limits.

Recognizing your limits you either restrain yourself, or you proceed rashly and pay the price.

♄: You exercise discipline to restrain yourself when you know you have limited resources.

♂: You tend to seek attention and approval from others, disregarding your own genuine ideals.

60.4 Extending: Using limitations as a natural springboard for growth.

You effectively cope with all restraints, or become depressed when you cannot get your way.

☿: You apply yourself to make the best of any situation by dealing with it directly.

♀: If you try to harmonize rather than surpass life's limitations you can easily become dejected.

60.5 Finding Inner-independence: Accepting any restrictions agreeably has great effect.

You live openly within acceptable restraints for yourself and others, or become hypocritical.

♆: Your intuitive nature knows natural boundaries that are acceptable for yourself and others.

♃: Your expansive nature has trouble in defining appropriate bounds for yourself and others.

60.6 Being Idealistic: Balancing between indulgence and unreasonable restraint.

You know that any excessive restraints imposed on you and others will meet with resentment.

⚷: Your innovative approach to handling restraints makes them easier to accept.

☿: You become overwhelmed by imposed limitations and can find yourself depressed.

61

中孚 **Inner Truth**

Sincerity : Mystery

Your innermost sincerity compels you towards what you know to be true.

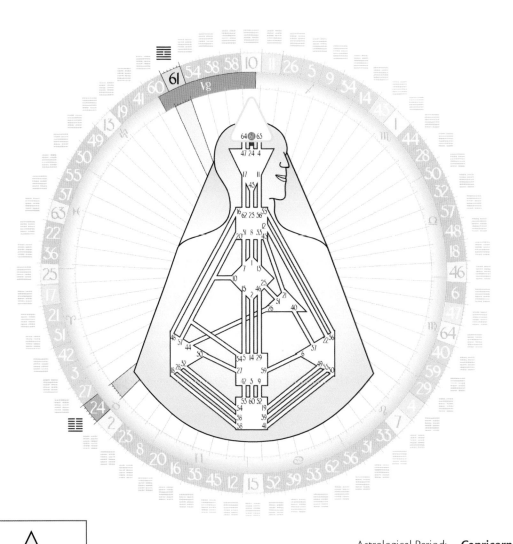

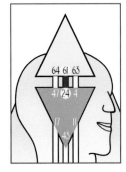

Part of Channel 61-24

The Channel of the Thinker

Center: **Crown**   Circuit: **Individual/ Knowing**

Astrological Period: **Capricorn** Ⅴ♐

Astrological Positions:

20°45'00" Ⅴ♐ – 26°22'30" Ⅴ♐

1:	20°45'00" Ⅴ♐ – 21°41'15" Ⅴ♐
2:	21°41'15" Ⅴ♐ – 22°37'30" Ⅴ♐
3:	22°37'30" Ⅴ♐ – 23°33'45" Ⅴ♐
4:	23°33'45" Ⅴ♐ – 24°30'00" Ⅴ♐
5:	24°30'00" Ⅴ♐ – 25°26'15" Ⅴ♐
6:	25°26'15" Ⅴ♐ – 26°22'30" Ⅴ♐

The pressure to know ...... and the eventual realization that your thoughts can lead you to glimpse truth but cannot maintain a hold on it.
Truth happens in a silent mind.
Psychosis
Disenchanted ◇ Mad : Inspiration :: Sanctity

61.1 Having Perception: Quietly allowing your psychic attunement.

You have the means to probe deeply into some of the inner workings of life.

Ψ: Your mystical nature is attuned to be able to align many cosmic and earthly realities.

♀: If you are so keen to align with esoteric realms you lose touch with your everyday realities.

61.2 Shining Light: Finding the thread of truth in anything.

You either have the inner development to contain your compelling inspirations, or not.

☾: You have the gift to inspire others through an attunement to your own clear well-being.

♂: You know that you shine brightly but have difficulty in handling others' recognition of that.

61.3 Remaining Inner-dependent: Staying true in your own life.

You trust yourself in all interactions while acknowledging how easily you are affected by others.

☾: You attune to all relationships that allow your truth and inspirations to flourish.

♂: It is easy for others to misunderstand you and you often find you have become estranged.

61.4 Holding Higher Truth: Following your clarity to find resonant truth in others.

You seek the truth in any situation whether you are inspired from within or from other people.

♄: Your disciplined nature holds you in your process until truth is revealed, regardless...

♃: Any attempt to seek truth outside of yourself will result in you becoming disillusioned.

61.5 Being Ingenious: Uniting everyone by interpreting truth innovatively.

Abiding by your principles you impart truth to others, whether they accept it easily or not.

♄: Your discipline and ingenuity to know the truth is unaffected if others embrace you or not.

♂: You insist on being accepted for your stance in life and your interpretations of truth.

61.6 Being Insightful: Universal expressions of truth are not always recognized.

Expressing your truth through personal experiences can inspire others practically or not.

(☊): Sincerely adapting your truth as a tangible reality has a great effect on others.

♂: You alienate others by pushing them to adopt your impractical grasp of truth.

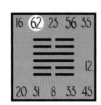

小過 Expressed Details
Clarification
Much ado about anything as you express and define details that are of value to the present and the future.

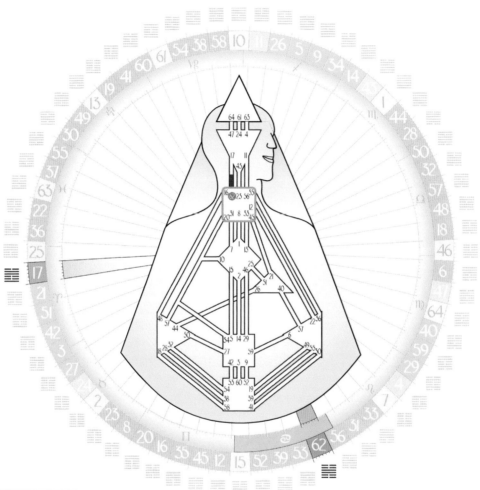

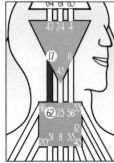

Part of Channel 17-62
The Channel of the Organizer

Center: **Throat**   Circuit: **Collective/Logic**

Astrological Period: **Cancer** ♋

Astrological Positions:

	20°45'00" ♋ – 26°22'30" ♋
1:	20°45'00" ♋ – 21°41'15" ♋
2:	21°41'15" ♋ – 22°37'30" ♋
3:	22°37'30" ♋ – 23°33'45" ♋
4:	23°33'45" ♋ – 24°30'00" ♋
5:	24°30'00" ♋ – 25°26'15" ♋
6:	25°26'15" ♋ – 26°22'30" ♋

Your logical organization of all matters in life becomes possible through attending to all pertinent and relevant details. When you express logical thoughts it does not mean that they are always completely correct or have to be acted on...they are just logical thoughts.

Intellect

Obsessive ◇ Pedantic : Precision :: Impeccability

62.1 Being Practical: Proceeding towards what is attainable and aligned.

If you confine yourself to essential details in life you are well prepared for many challenges.

♆: Your gift of imagination will always enhance the potentially mundane aspects in your life.

♂: You express your plans as actions with the possibility of talking your way into trouble.

62.2 Being Sensible: Reaching out to give and receive aid.

You always find that needed assistance is available if you persevere diligently in your own way.

♃: Staying with your process you give help when needed and receive help when it is offered.

☿: You have an anxiety that is hard to restrain when you consider yourself bound by traditions.

62.3 Being Unassuming: Recognizing the need to downplay a tendency for overconfidence.

Your good judgment, common sense and preparedness always prevail in difficult situations.

⚷: Innovation and conscientiousness allows you to find relevant details in all aspects of life.

♀: Imposing your need for harmony over everything else can cause you to act unreasonably.

62.4 Being Patient: Being watchful for principled opportunities.

You accept the need to be cautious especially in situations when you see yourself as right.

♀: With your particular sensitivity you observe how life is enhanced by discreet interventions.

☊: Seeing ways to transform every area of life you push for opportunities to be assertive.

62.5 Being Considerate: Planning, preparation and performance.

When everything is in place there comes a time of identifying when and how things proceed.

☾: When you move steadily from one state to another you align details with outcomes.

♆: You are often ready to move on in life but continue to remain lost in your imagination.

62.6 Accepting Limits: Recognizing practical limitations in all your endeavors.

You need to exercise reserve if you are going to interact within the scope of your abilities.

♄: You discipline yourself to remain clear in your intentions when confronted by limits in life.

☿: You have the intellect to appreciate your limits, but often lack the intent to maintain them.

既濟 Doubts
Critical perception
(After Completion)
Constantly refreshing your view in a world where there is always change.

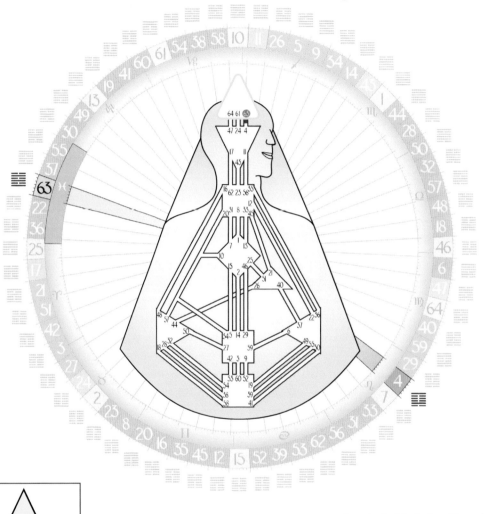

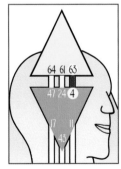

Part of Channel 63-4
Channel of the Logical Mind

Center: **Crown**   Circuit: **Collective/Logic**

Astrological Period: **Pisces** ♓

Astrological Positions:

	11°22'30" ♓ – 17°00'00" ♓
1:	11°22'30" ♓ – 12°18'45" ♓
2:	12°18'45" ♓ – 13°15'00" ♓
3:	13°15'00" ♓ – 14°01'15" ♓
4:	14°01'15" ♓ – 15°07'30" ♓
5:	15°07'30" ♓ – 16°03'45" ♓
6:	16°03'45" ♓ – 17°00'00" ♓

Your gift of critical perception needs forever tempering and attuning with its present environment. Fulfillment is attained through recognizing that ultimately everything is in its right place and order... and that no one likes to be personally criticized even if you are pressured to comment on their lives.

Doubt

Self-doubting ⟨⟩ Suspicious : Inquiry :: Truth

63.1 Investigating: Constantly reviewing your circumstances.
You either retain or lose your poise as the effects of your achievements become apparent.

☉: You are not overly distracted by the pressures that accompany achievements.

♂: Continuously analyzing your life you still seem to chase unnecessary achievements.

63.2 Being Reserved: Remaining steadfast in your life quest for personal integrity.
You hold true to your aims through difficult times whether you impress others or not.

♃: You can share your doubts with others while never letting go of your own inherent purpose.

☋: Being vulnerable in difficulties leads you sometimes to doubt your own and others' purposes.

63.3 Revitalizing: Considering high ideals in all matters.
You eventually find out how to attain your goals and see who and what can help you.

♃: The pressure to achieve compels you through profound doubts over your aims and allies.

♄: Sometimes you are rigid with yourself and others when pursuing your objectives.

63.4 Being Clear: Remaining alert for potential disturbances to your fulfillment.
By describing your thought processes to others you alleviate any doubts in a timely fashion.

☿: You quickly anticipate any potential complications in life so that they are resolved easily.

♂: You can be overconfident in resolving problems and tend to make hasty decisions.

63.5 Being Beneficent: Considering sincerity above showiness.
Great achievements are possible if you candidly examine your doubts and actions on the way.

☉: You implement a deliberately helpful plan while analyzing every aspect of your process.

♂: You might easily forget to have a heartfelt celebration when you complete your endeavors.

63.6 Anticipating: When completing anything remain present and looking forwards.
Dragging your mind out of past situations into the present is a lifelong awareness process.

♃: You move on in life when you accept current resolutions and leave old doubts behind.

☊: If you insist on regurgitating old issues you will keep 'spinning' them in new ways.

64

未濟

Diverse Possibilities
Confusion (Before Completion)
In expansion, there is no perfect equilibrium and no absolute correctness, and yet there is always the pressure to find a balance.

64 61 63

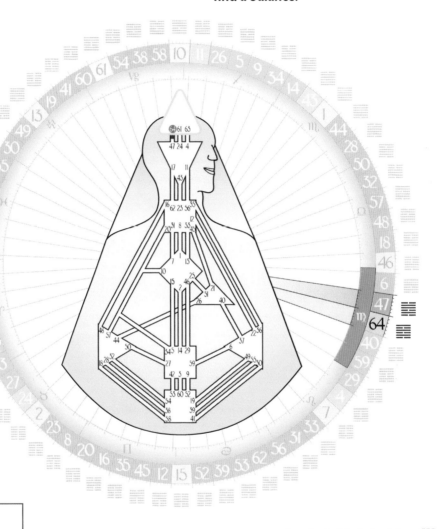

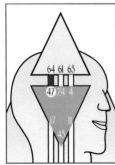

64 61 63

47 24 4

17 43

Part of Channel 64-47
The Channel of Abstract Thinking

Center: **Crown**   Circuit: **Collective/Sensing**

Astrological Period: **Virgo** ♍

Astrological Positions:

11°22'30" ♍ – 17°00'00" ♍

1:   11°22'30" ♍ – 12°18'45" ♍
2:   12°18'45" ♍ – 13°15'00" ♍
3:   13°15'00" ♍ – 14°01'15" ♍
4:   14°01'15" ♍ – 15°07'30" ♍
5:   15°07'30" ♍ – 16°03'45" ♍
6:   16°03'45" ♍ – 17°00'00" ♍

Life and our experiencing of Existence is a self-fulfilling journey that continues to move to completion, entering into and through new cycles and spirals. In seeking to find a perfect answer to life, look into the stars and try to choose your favorite…! There is always more!

Confusion

Imitating ⟷ Confusion : Imagination :: Illumination

64.1 Transitioning: Inner resolve leads you towards fulfilling outcomes.
Relying solely on past perspectives of your life experiences will not bring you fulfillment.

♀: Your inner harmony gives patience and forbearance without promising satisfying outcomes.

♂: You are ready to act in any instant when things seem to be resolved, but often are not.

64.2 Being Dedicated: Remaining true to your inner voice.
Trusting in yourself and in your own process you find your clarity and make your moves.

♀: Relying on your inner harmony you wait for an inner sense that precedes resolution.

☾: You attune with many aspects of life sometimes over-committing yourself unnecessarily.

64.3 Restarting: Commencing anew when old ways no longer apply.
You need to be clear from the outset in any endeavors and recognize who else has that clarity.

♄: When you wait for renewed clarity and perception you deliberately transcend confusion.

☾: Being out of touch with the times you commit to strategies without fulfilling outcomes.

64.4 Overcoming: All inner struggles require persistence and determination.
You need inner principles to transcend confusion and clarify how you are going to proceed.

☾: You review all cycles of life with a certainty that sooner or later you will find realization.

♂: With an overly energized mind you find that confusion never clears for very long.

64.5 Being Exemplary: Constantly persistent, you shine brightly from an inner resolve.
You realize that your inner light can be shone outwards to disperse other people's confusions.

♀: Your steadfast inner harmony reaches outwards to shed light on the world's confusion.

♃: You see possibilities for clarification but tend to be overburdened by others' confusions.

64.6 Keeping Your Head: Remaining lucid in celebrating achievements.
You celebrate with clarity or lapse into self-indulgence when confusions are resolved.

☿: Your patient brilliance allows you to sort through any amount of chaos and find resolutions.

♀: You delight in embracing disorders but ultimately may get lost in the ensuing chaos.

How to use the Book of Lines as a modern day oracle, or contemporary version of the *IChing*

Your first step: Assemble necessary materials

For this process, you will need:
- A notebook or your journal and an ink pen
- Three coins of the same type (whatever coins you use, just make sure they are the same size and same weight)
- A comfortable and quiet place to sit
- A surface to write on

Your second step: The Question

Tune into your question, to get to the essence of it. Expressing it clearly at the onset is as important as receiving the answer with equanimity. For instance, if you are inclined to ask, "When will I ever meet my soulmate?", and you take a little time to go deeper with that question, you will see it is full of nuances that could go in many directions…

"Why have I not met my soulmate thus far in life?"

"Am I actually meant to have a soulmate, or not?"

"Will the fact that I meet my soulmate at some point in the future ensure that we will recognize each other?"

Asking a more focused question that gets to the real heart of the matter will result in better chances of your receiving an answer that resonates with you and provides valuable guidance.

In our example, if you ask instead, "What do I need to know, learn or do, to draw my soulmate to me within the next 12 months?" You will receive a more focused and empowering answer.

"Yes" or "no" questions, those too broad in scope, and "either/or" questions are not productive. If you keep your questions focused on the result of a particular choice or course of action on your part, or the outcome of reaching toward a particular goal or relationship, the answers you receive will be much more relevant and useful.

Once you have clearly formulated your question, write it down. This will further help you focus your intent upon receiving an answer that is specific as possible.

Your third step: Set your Intention and Remain Open

Now that you have clearly formulated your question, use whatever ritual resonates with you, whether that be prayer, meditation, symbols, calling in the Light, or a specific ritual like, candle-lighting, to align your intent to receive the highest and clearest guidance possible. Ask to receive only that which will be for your Highest Good and the Highest Good of all concerned.

It is important to remain open to universal wisdom, rather than being attached to receiving a specific answer or outcome that you may wish… who knows, something much better may be on the way to you.

Relax into the process, trusting your ability to tap into universal wisdom and guidance.

Your fourth step: Throwing the coins

We use the coins to represent the binary nature of life on earth, yin and yang. "Heads" (the side of the coin that typically has the picture of someone's head on it) is a **yang** coin, while "Tails" (the other side of the coin that has an image with nothing remotely like a picture of a head on it) is a **yin** coin. For each time you consult *The Book of Lines* on a specific issue, you will be doing a total of six throwings of the three coins to yield your answer. This will come to be interpreted in the form of a hexagram.

Keeping your question in mind, place the coins in your hands, cup your hands together covering the coins completely, shake your cupped hands and then throw the coins onto a hard surface. This first roll of the coins indicates the first, or bottom line, of the hexagram. (see illustration below) When the coins land, notice and write down the combinations of yin and yang, as such:

A "yang" coin is "heads."   A "yin" coin is "tails."

If you throw **two heads and one tail,** the line is yang, or solid : ———————— . If you throw **two tails and one head,** the line is yin, or broken : ——— ——— .

If you throw all three of the same type of coin, this is called a "changing line", and you proceeds thus:

If you throw **three heads,** the line starts as yang, marked: ——— o ——— "changing" to yin ——— ——— .

If you throw **three tails,** the line start as yin, marked: ▬▬ x ▬▬ "changing" to yang ▬▬▬▬ .

Whether you have changing lines or not, the first part of the reading is the same:

Throw six times, and after each throw, write down, from the bottom up, the combination of lines thrown. Here's an example:

What do I need to know or do, to ensure my new project will be successful?

6. ▬▬ ▬▬

5. ▬▬ ▬▬   Upper Trigram

4. ▬▬ ▬▬

3. ▬▬▬▬▬

2. ▬▬ ▬▬   Lower Trigram

1. ▬▬ ▬▬

In this example, there were no changing lines, so you will simply go directly to the text for the answer.

Your fifth step: Finding the hexagram, and consulting the text

Look inside the back cover at the colored square diagram containing hexagram numbers.

Each hexagram is divided into a two groups of three: the "Lower Lines" and the "Upper Lines." The Lower Lines run in the column down the side of the square diagram, and the "Upper Lines" across the top.

Find the "Lower Lines" from your first three throws of the coins, (from the bottom, up). Make a note of the row (or the name) of that Trigram. Then, find the corresponding upper Trigram on the top row, across the page. Draw an imaginary line from the Trigram in the top row, down to meet the imaginary line extended horizontally from the Trigram in the left side row. The box at the intersection will contain the Hexagram number which holds your answer.

In the case of our example question, (Ken in the left column combines with K'un in the top row), where the two rows intersect in the diagram, it shows that the answer is contained within Hexagram 15.

15 is called Humanity, Extremes. You read the Meaning and the Commentary on the pages for Hexagram/Gate 15 in the Book of Lines.

With this answer, you are being directed to pay attention to your role in the interactions you have with all the different people and living forms, in all levels of personal acquaintance or society who come into and out of your life.

Changing Lines

In the case where one or several of the coin throws yields either three yang or three yin coins, we have what is called, "Changing Lines." In this case, the hexagram formed by the original six throws of the coins is read first, to understand the situation as is, then a second step is taken, to read how the situation in question, or the outcome one is inquiring about, may be unfolding. Here's an example of how to proceed when you throw one or more "changing lines":

6. ————————			6. ————————	
5. ————————	Upper Trigram		5. ————————	
4. ————————			4. ————————	
3. ——— x ———	(three tails) changes to:		3. ————————	
2. ————————	Lower Trigram		2. ————————	
1. ——— ———			1. ——— ———	

In this example, the third line changes from yin to yang, revealing the next hexagram to read after reading the first one thrown. In this case:

- A. Read the first hexagram, which in this example is: Hexagram 6, Conflict Resolution, Emotional Balance. Read the Meaning and Commentary as usual, to get the overall reflection on your question, then, because the changing line is the third line, read that line: Hexagram 6, Line 3:

  "Having Reservations : Resolutions often happen by playing a passive role. Achieving emotional clarity comes by making and breaking commitments with alertness."

- B. Next, read the new hexagram produced by the changing line, in this case, Hexagram 6, with the changing line in the third place, becomes, Hexagram 44 :

  Patterns, Meeting Together. Read the general text to understand how the situation in question is unfolding. This text contains the final answer, or outcome, to your question.

If there is more than one changing line in your hexagram, be sure to read each of those changing lines in the original hexagram, along with its general commentary, then proceed to the next hexagram. For example, if in the above example of arriving at the original hexagram, you had an additional changing line, because you threw:

6. ————————	Upper Trigram	6. ————————
5. ——— o ———	(three heads) changes to:	5. ——— — ———
4. ————————		4. ————————
3. ——— x ———	(three tails) changes to:	3. ————————
2. ————————	Lower Trigram	2. ————————
1. ——— — ———		1. ——— — ———

In this example, we begin with the same hexagram, but in addition to the third line changing from yin to yang (marked as a "x"), we also have the fifth line changing from yang to yin, (marked as an "o"), revealing an entirely different next hexagram to read after reading the first one thrown.

In this case, you would first read Hexagram 6 and its commentary, then read the 6.3 line commentary and the 6.5 line commentary, before moving on to read the new hexagram created by the two changing lines, which is: Hexagram 50.

Your sixth step: Interpreting the Answer

The Book of Lines was written both as a guide for use in interpreting your Human Design Life Chart, as well as a stand-alone modern day oracle that can serve as a clear reflection from the perspective of Universal Wisdom, as it applies to our modern day circumstances, and more highly developed personal awareness. That said, it retains its original gift as an oracle, and as such, its answers are given in symbolic form, designed to stimulate your unconscious, subconscious and superconscious mind, to bring a broader perspective in your life.

To benefit fully from the answers supplied in The Book of Lines, begin the process as suggested, by "setting space", opening to divine wisdom, and becoming receptive to universal language, and the meaning of the text will then "dawn upon you" as you read and may continue to reveal more nuances in the days following your question. Sometimes it may seem that your question has not directly been answered, but if you remain open, you will discover that the Book of Lines has given you a look into a deeper level of understanding, or a "heads-up" about a situation that you may have otherwise entirely missed.

UPPER LINES ▶ LOWER LINES ▼	CHI'EN	CHEN	K'AN	KEN	K'UN	SUN	LI	TUI
CHIEN	1	34	5	26	11	9	14	43
CHEN	25	51	3	27	24	42	21	17
K'AN	6	40	29	4	7	59	64	47
KEN	33	62	39	52	15	53	56	31
K'UN	12	16	8	23	2	20	35	45
SUN	44	32	48	18	46	57	50	28
LI	13	55	63	22	36	37	30	49
TUI	10	54	60	41	19	61	38	58

Printed in Poland
by Amazon Fulfillment
Poland Sp. z o.o., Wrocław

32518926R00094